/people

AT HOME IN MORE THAN
ONE DISCIPLINE

/people

AT HOME IN MORE THAN
ONE DISCIPLINE

THEO LORENZ
TANJA SIEMS

MIRAJ AHMED
AMR ASSAAD
DAVID GREENE
GRAHAM HARMAN
ROBIN HUNT
PORTIA KAMONS
ALBENA YANEVA

4   Content Overview / people
8   Overview of the Projects

10   **INTRODUCTION**
      David Greene

CHAPTER 1
16   **ORIGINS**
      Miraj Ahmed, Theo Lorenz and Tanja Siems

18   On the question of the definition of Architecture
20   On the question of the 'Art World'
21   On the question of Enabler and Creator
24   On the question of Education
24   On the question of Format
25   On the question of Design
25   On the question of responsibility of creativity
28   On the question of funding in changing economic landscapes
28   On the question of innovation
29   On the question of networks and collaboration
31   Concluding paragraph

CHAPTER 2
32   **CREATION THROUGH OUT OF THICK AIR APPROACH**
      Theo Lorenz and Tanja Siems

34   The motivation of creativity
35   /people
42   From 'A Priori' to 'Out of Thick Air'
42   Matter of Facts
43   Matters of Moderation
43   Matter of Concerns: Design of the Design Process
44   Out of Thick Air
48   Projects within established frameworks or grants
49   Projects hosted within a specific local or political setting
49   Projects as host
54   Projects of overlapping frequencies
54   A feasible approach to creativity
58   Can we work together?
61   How we work together
62   Conclusion

CHAPTER 3

64 THE NETWORKED STUDIO

Albena Yaneva, Theo Lorenz and Tanja Siems

66	Agency and Interprofessional Collaborations
67	The Spaces that Make us Think
70	How is the AAIS organised and how it works?
72	Inter-professionalism in Action
72	No Genius, but Collectives
77	Learning Based on Evidence and Shared Experience
77	Building Skills for Expanding Networks
86	Space as a Narrative
87	Bridging the Divide between Performing Subjects and Stage Objects
87	Expanding the Networks
92	Networks of the Past – Networks of the Future
92	Bringing People Together through Design
93	Tools and Techniques
94	Ecological Concerns
95	Conclusions

CHAPTER 4

98 PERFORMANCE, PROTEST, POLITICS

Robin Hunt, Portia Kamons, Theo Lorenz and Tanja Siems

100	The importance of performance
102	Performance presentation
106	Performative elements of presentations
113	Case studies of political activism
120	Protest
121	'Stepping in' and 'stepping up'
124	Politics

CHAPTER 5

126   **OBJECTS AND PERFORMANCE**

Graham Harman and Theo Lorenz

132   Architecture, Design and Performance
137   Bad Objects
138   Minimal or absent design in performance
139   The Acting of Objects
143   Urban Performance and Objects
146   Performance as Object of Protest and Politics

CHAPTER 6

148   **BEHIND THE SCENES**

Theo Lorenz and Tanja Siems

151   Areas of research
155   People
155   How we meet
157   Helping hands and mind
157   The mundane, anecdotal and serendipitous
160   How we concentrate
160   iPhone Tower
161   Out of your comfort zone
164   Moments of creation and success
164   How we celebrate
165   Creative participatory places
172   Elements as light and projections
172   Senses and haptic habitat
173   Audience participation
176   Notations as a communicator
177   Creative accounting

7

CHAPTER 7

182 **COMPASSION, COLLABORATION AND CREATIVITY**
Theo Lorenz and Tanja Siems

184 Responsibility in Design
184 Compassion as an act of creativity
186 Don't look away
186 Othering
187 Fields of intervention
187 Project Briefs
188 "Common Ground", Intellectual Empathy and "After-effect"
192 Culinary Cultures
193 The self-righteous trap

CHAPTER 8

196 **SPACES OF OPPORTUNITY**
Amr Assaad and Theo Lorenz

198 A Home for /People
198 Framing a New Environment
199 Making and Meeting
202 Re-imagining the Club
203 Contemporary Collaborations
206 Infrastructure and Invitation
207 Designing for Plurality
211 /Person and /Practice
211 Economic Structures and Generosity
214 Timeliness and Context
215 Continuity and Composition

222 **ACKNOWLEDGEMENTS**

CRASH BOOM BAU 2009
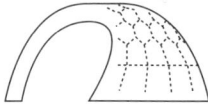

SEED TO SCENE 2010
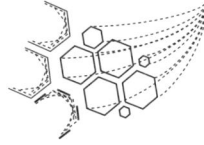

EXQUISITE CORPSE 2011
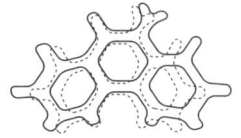

LOVE HAS NEVER BEEN...2025
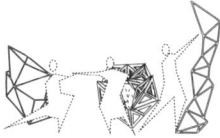

BORNE 2024

MOULT 2023

ECHO 2022
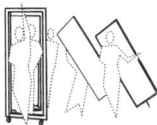

ORIGIN 2021

SCREAM OUT LOUD! 2020
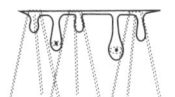

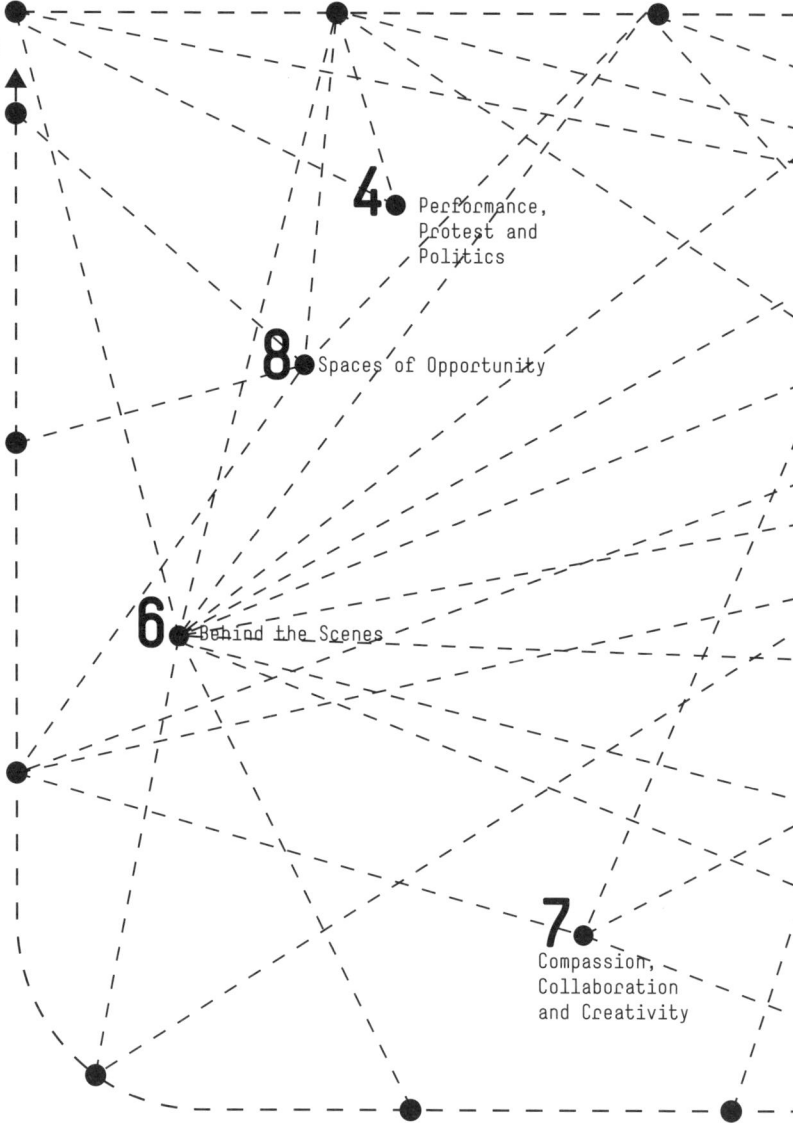

4 Performance, Protest and Politics

8 Spaces of Opportunity

6 Behind the Scenes

7 Compassion, Collaboration and Creativity

ANGLES OF INCIDENCE 2012

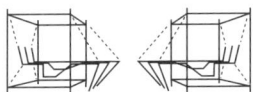

FLOW FIELDS 2013

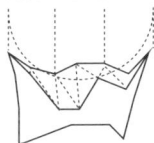

THE CONVERSATION 2014

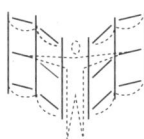

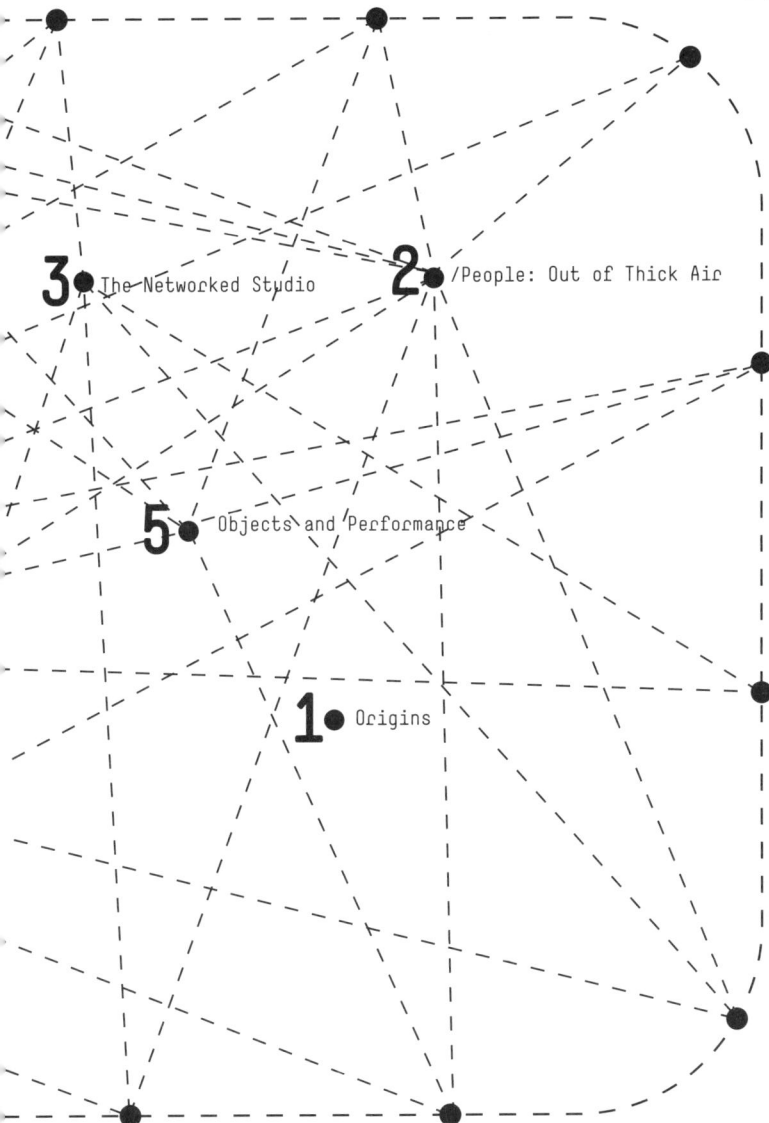

3 The Networked Studio

2 /People: Out of Thick Air

5 Objects and Performance

1 Origins

MOVING STONE 2015

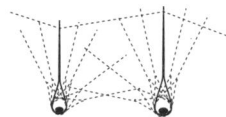

UnREAL:XYZ 2016

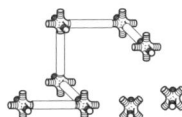

TRUST,TRUTH INTEGRITY 2017

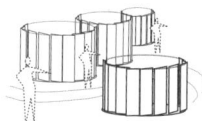

PORTRAIT OF HUMANS 2019

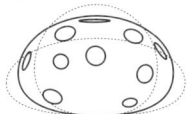

A WALK 2018

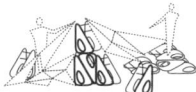

David Greene

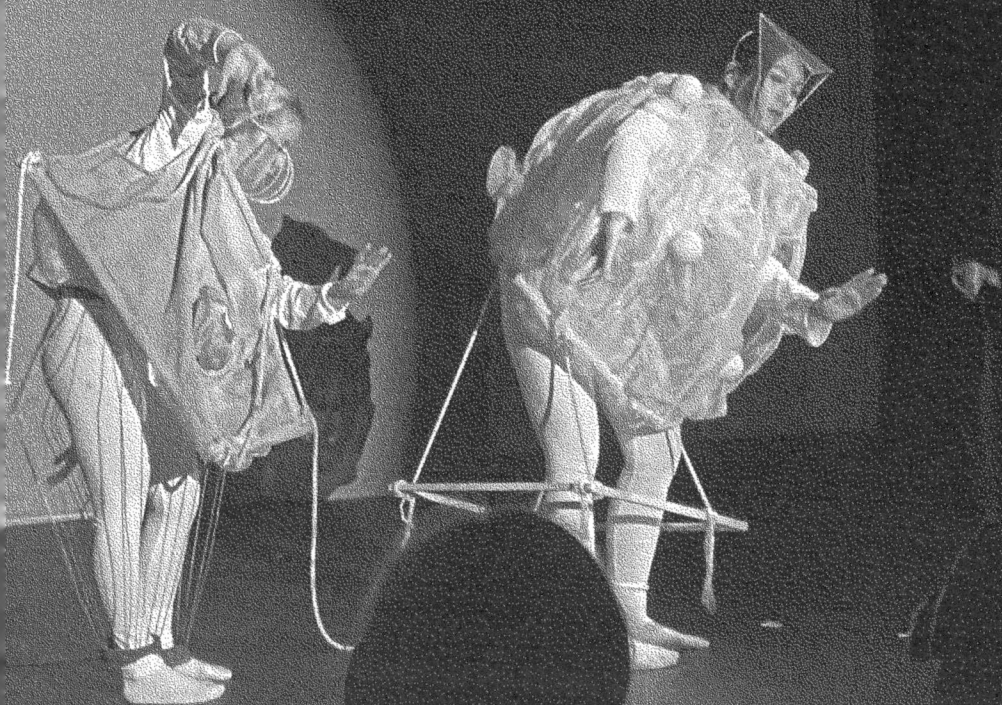

INTRODUCTION

This book gives indications about how the AAIS explores some of the new questions facing architecture and particularly how these might be responded to in new forms of design education.

At the turn of the millennium, the belief in spectacular architecture infects architectural education in so many imaginations.

However, fed by a new global interconnectedness, by new technologies that are an extension of our consciousness, neglected issues emerge. The need to acknowledge the relation between architecture and society, the financial conditions of its production increase as the belief in spectacular form begins to be questioned.

There is growing necessity to see architecture as part of the planet's ecosystem.

New ideas for how architecture can be studied are demanded so these notes concentrate on the nature of the subject of the book, the course itself, and the context in which it lives, and perhaps the need to see design not as a body of knowledge but as a way of thinking, particularly also as a way of behaviour, as a recent AAIS graduate reminded me *"I would say that the AAIS treats architecture as a discipline rather than a practice, where we are all students of architecture, rather than architecture students. ..."*

McLuhan claimed that media have turned the classroom into a feudal dungeon. Here located in a school of architecture, the AAIS is one room, a room he may have understood. A windowless room, a room more like a stage, an apparatus, flexible, nearly a black cube. Something may happen or may not, a challenge to the sepulchral silence and alienation of the computer studio.

Does the multiple authorship of the book question an architectural education associated with a cult individuality?

Can this book serve as a potential paradigm — a blueprint for a school of architecture, not architecture. A paradigm examined in the AAIS through the design and production of poetic performances.

With deference to Krauss, within these pages, we might discern the emergence of architectural learning in the expanded field.

Alan Kaprow invented the Happening, Vito Acconci claims architecture is not about space but time. The AAIS programme claims these two influences and the necessity of a collaborative working method, aspiring to respond to an era where established norms and methods face an influx of fresh intelligence, does this book emerge as a manual of possibilities in a culture demanding participation and involvement.

Performance, the intersection of protest and politics, the dynamic of objects in motion, the concealed machinery behind the scenes.
For Krauss, the expanded field grants the artist, and by extension, the AAIS, the liberty to draw from any medium deemed essential.

In a conversation with a student of the AAIS, we pondered on the essence of architecture as a choreography through space, with the drawing serving as a sort of architectural score – a navigational chart through the realms of design.
Does the AAIS privilege the claim that architecture is choreography, is events, and uses the design of the performance as a paradigm to explore this in its dark not-a-classroom.

Here the Architectural Association, by supporting the experiments of the AAIS, in the junctures between, art, architecture and performance, reaffirms its reputation for pushing boundaries , of inventing new categories of design learning action. The assertion of a new connectedness suggests that architectural education can't ignore that architecture is made of a weave between multiple professions, a confluence of work and network. A hidden worknet that underpins all architectural projects.
This publication should encourage a new generation of architectural schools and thinkers to design their own paths through this expanded field.

In 2007 artist Alex Schweder, coined the term 'Performance Architecture', breathing new life into the Happening? Google gives this practice's key words as: Critical Spatial Practice, Interdisciplinarity, Architecture, Politics of Space, Theatre Architecture, words that the AAIS may be familiar with.
Author Branko Kolarevic has suggested ...today, digital quantitative and qualitative performance-based simulation represents the technological foundation of the emerging performative architecture.
Does the AAIS recognise any synergy with his words, we must ask them, for new technology is making new alliances, AAIS reaches out to a critique of current architectural educational orthodoxies. Or maybe it is something less complicated, something that inspires as a current student suggests. ...As a pedagogy it brings in the notion of thinking about thinking. ...a one sentence curriculum?

0.1
Punk theatre performance dEAD
LABOUR at the AAIS studio
alongside Harry Waters a homage
to Pink Floyd's 1966 performance
at the same venue (TL)

0.2/3
David Greene at the Workshop
review "Jazz Music Bar", James
Baldwin's Harlem in the
1950s led by Mona Camille
and Renaud Wiser (TL)

0.4/5
Results of the weeklong Interprofessional Studio
session on „compassion" and „intellectual
empathy" based on the concept and
article by Theo Lorenz and Tanja Siems (TL)

0.6
Flexible arrangements of the AAIS
studio space here the Network
Theory seminar session with
Theo Lorenz and Tanja Siems (TL)

1

Miraj Ahmed
Theo Lorenz
Tanja Siems

ORIGINS

Origins

New ways of thinking and working do not derive from single ideas, strategies, or planning. Nor do they necessarily emerge from chance, serendipity, or the practical need for a gap to be filled. The origins of new educational methodologies are often the result of overlaps between all these elements as well as, of course, evolution. One starts with a critical standpoint and a field of questions. 'Why can't we do this?' and 'What if we can do that' punctuate freely associated loose conversation. Basically, these slowly evolve in the overlaps of needs, possibilities and initiatives that begin to emerge and form outline areas of investigation, with a loose set of parameters that raise further questions addressing possible new methodologies. The creation of a space for new ways of thinking and working requires a lot of thinking. Investigations may show that certain educational models are perhaps not new in themselves, however, opportunities and innovations in new approaches lie in the links and connections between them. Overlaps and commonalities allow the possibility of further investigation and the development of verifiable evidence of a way forward.

There are difficulties in the formulation of a clear product, description or even ambition within known parameters and benchmarks for educational models, particularly when clearly defined genres, approaches and concepts never capture the unknown and emerging. With no clearly defined precedents, or evidence, case studies need to be produced to sustain an argument and to prove a concept. One must continually find clearly definable shapes within the thick fog of possibilities, moments of verifiable incidences that raise further questions. This evolutionary approach of questioning, testing, and proving through creative application is simultaneously the origin and the continued story of the Interprofessional Studio. It is its core modus operandi. A continued quest for initiatives and overlaps within the creative fields to find answers to the questions of our times through proven evidence of applied projects.

The Architectural Association in London, with its own mythical origin story, has been the incubator to raise these questions throughout its history. The AA, a private school of architecture, was founded to provide an alternative architectural apprenticeship in 1847. By 1890, it had established itself, leading the way in architectural education. Its focus has always been architecture and its independence as an association allowed it to be a laboratory of ideas. It is well known as a space of discussion and radical projects and in its various eras produced highly influential practitioners. The institution is connected to a global arena of architectural discourse. It has seen a changing pedagogy in its lifetime, in which all its constituents are participatory members of a school community, a democratic system where everyone has a vote. If one looks at other legendary educational establishments such as the Bauhaus or Black Mountain College, it is possible to see certain relationships. One can attribute the origin of the 'unit' system to the AA. In this construct, the Unit Masters and Tutors lead a studio of students through a year-long design research project, in which they were exploring in particular architectural theories. Within its environment of cultural research topics such as history, philosophy, sociology, science, and art have always been encouraged to explore these important matters through architectural projects. The school has always been porous to other disciplines and its output has often reached beyond the conventional definitions of architecture.

Freedom entrusted to the educators has meant that within the school there is a variety of pedagogical approaches that are open to outside influence, but all directed to the pursuit of Architecture. Students make their way through the undergrad and post-grad school with a liberal education on their way to becoming practising architects. However, as tutors in Foundation, we were not constrained by the need to fulfil the requirements of architectural education. The students are like creative stem cells and could become anything. Consequently, the idea of a space in which students can nurture their creative practice without streaming towards a particular discipline at a later stage in the school became a discussion point a 'what if'. A space in which questions can be posed about different disciplinary methodologies and the overlaps that happen between them. The school, with its association of students, staff, practitioners, and its creative and technical infrastructure, is an ideal space for those who do not wish to become architects but who may benefit creatively and professionally from engaging with its ecosystem temporarily. Such a space would also fertilise the school as a kind of open studio of unfettered research.

These questions are still open, and present, and in many cases, have intensified immensely. We cannot claim to have discovered generalisable answers and solutions, but the open approach has produced proven evidence and lasting after-effects for specific projects, groups, and individuals. As creatives who see themselves at home between fine art, architecture and education, our core discussion throughout the years focused on the following core questions.

The question of the definition of Architecture and the 'Art World'
The question of Enabler and Creator
The question of Education, Format and Design
The question of responsibility of creativity within changing political and social landscapes
The question of funding in changing economic landscapes
The question of innovation, of networks and collaboration

On the question of the definition of Architecture
The Architectural Association has from the outset, been a place of extraordinary experimental and participatory work. Throughout its history, it defined its work far beyond the traditional classification of Architecture and the built environment. Performance and applied creative work have at all times been an integrated part of the dynamic and innovative character of the school and created pivotal moments within its history such as the spectacular installations by Bernard Tschumi in 1974, the AA carnival extravaganza in 1978, as well as being a springboard for architects such as Rem Koolhaas and Zaha Hadid. The Architectural Association has also produced some of the most influential and creative artists and creatives beyond the discipline of Architecture, for example, the world-renowned stage designer Mark Fisher, the industrial designer Ron Arad and even in its early days the renowned writer Thomas Hardy.

The school has always taken a critical and open stance on the definition of Architecture and architectural education. Its independence has meant that it can be responsive to contemporary cultural issues. The definition of architecture is seen as fluid and relates to the politics, economics, and cultural shifts through time. AAIS emerged at the end of an era of intense interest in the possibilities and production of form within architecture. The global economic downturn during the years 2007 and 2008 saw a rejection of building 'iconic' architecture and the phenomena of 'starchitects' with a renewed interest in performative political space, where innovation is achieved through economy and participatory creativity. It has become imperative that architecture addresses the contemporary issues of climate crisis and socio-political atomisation.

Today the tradition of a broad approach to creative and innovative work is visible throughout the AA school and within the public programme, with its wide range of lectures, exhibitions, and events and performances throughout the creative disciplines and arts. However, even in such an environment that constantly challenges fixed definitions of Architecture, restrictions and requirements for the disciplines are apparent. This became apparent in the Thames Gateway Exhibition called "Assembly" created by Theo Lorenz and Peter Staub in collaboration with the Diploma14 students (Barth 2006, p 67-71). New experimental approaches and research with an extended definition of Architecture are necessary to continue to innovate and extend the disciplines into the creative fields. Within this unique tradition of investigative and exploratory methods, the AAIS studio was established by Theo Lorenz and Tanja Siems in 2008 to extend and innovate the field of transdisciplinary work through applied projects.

On the question of the 'Art World'

Not dissimilar to the world of Architecture, the field of Fine Art seems increasingly limited, rather than enabled through what is loosely described as the 'Art World'. It struck us throughout the years, that separation, rather than an embracing approach, formed the fast-changing 'markets' of the Arts. Fast-changing headlines and trends set and reset the definition of art, privileging the work of curators, collectors, and galleries over the artists, with an emphasis on quick ideas, concepts and intents, rather than artistic uniqueness, after-effects, and critique. The artist, and art, in such an environment is getting limited, used and burned out. However, rather than submit to these artificial frameworks and limitations, we seek to create new settings in which the overlap of the arts and new disciplinary definitions can be found as well as old virtues of art rediscovered. In such a setting the 'opus' of the single artist is no longer set in isolation but rather brought back into constant negotiation. Fine art becomes active and transformative beyond its 'world' and in turn is reinstated with a lasting status.

The practice of art within the context of architecture is an interesting question. Historically, architects were trained in the art of drawing, painting, and sculpting, and the separation between disciplines is relatively new. In examining the practices of many contemporary artists, we can see that there is an interest and hunger in working more architecturally. Artists might extend their skill sets to incorporate spatial and structural techniques or they may collaborate with architects to realise their ideas. These scenarios generally happen mainly outside the context of education. Unfortunately, the training for collaborative working seems to happen in the professional world rather than the context of art school and its education as a creative process. An interesting trend in the art world at the present time is the practices that seem to cross over into unexpected disciplines, such as political or scientific research. Many artists work across a multitude of media, from painting to video, sculpture, and installation. In this regard, experts in fabrication are sought out in order to facilitate the realisation of works. For example, Adam Lowe set up Factum Arte in order to fulfil this need. Factum Arte are at the forefront of applied research and interdisciplinary practice within the art world, amassing a huge knowledge base of materials, fabrication techniques and artefact facsimile, for the purpose of fine art production as well as conservation.

On the question of Enabler and Creator
With this discourse comes the question of our individual status as creators, artists, and educators. In a world where everything is copyrighted, patented, and fixed, the question must be asked: how can artists and educators disseminate their work and knowledge whilst enlarging and enabling their own field of influence and work, rather than limiting and restricting it? An important form of behaviour is to overcome a definition of enabler and creator as separate entities but to simultaneously present their virtues within a network of equals, enabling and creating work at its best, with lasting effects.

The notion of enabler and creator can also be read in relation to the openness of techniques. We live in a time in which digital technology has meant that it is possible to have access to platforms that were previously inaccessible and required long periods of training. For example, the possibility and accessibility of filmmaking, from production to photography to editing is within easy grasp compared to 30 years ago. We can also understand the digital tools of enabling and creating in relation to collaboration. Digital tools have opened up the possibilities of creative collaboration on a global scale.

TL   Theo Lorenz
TS   Tanja Siems
TH   Takako Hasegawa
VB   Valerie Bennett
TZ   Tuitui Zhang
DK   Dongsoo Koo
SY   Sue_Jan_Yeong
AR   Alexandra Radounikli
KG   Patarita Tassanarapan
ZW   Zoie – Jie Wang
HW   Henrietta Williams
FA   Farah Aly
HM   Hadar Menkes
AL   Archlabyrinth Athen
PA   Parastoo Anoushehpour
JK   Jason Kofinas
YF   Yue Fu
OG   Oliviu Lugojan-Ghenciu

1.1
Project Review exhibition
of the Foundation Course
at the Architectural
Association 2005. (TL)

1.2
Performance "We fight our Battles with our Drawings on
the Wall" Tanja Siems and Theo Lorenz as part of the
166-year celebration of the Architectural Association
with Murray Lachlan Young. (VB)

1.3
Performers of New Movement
Collective and 'Young Movers' during
the performance with projection art
by Metamind Visuals. (VB)

1.4
AAIS "Salon" discussion with
Brett Steele, Mike Weinstock
as part of the "Bauhaus Lab"
2009 project. (TH)

On the question of Education

"The teacher learns the most..." is a statement we say a lot and use as a kind of litmus test against our own operation as educators, referring to Martin Heidegger (Heidegger 1954, p 15). This statement is not to be misunderstood; that an educator can be without knowledge. Rather, it states that good education should include one's own curiosity and ambition to widen knowledge, constantly re-evaluate it and seek to embark on a process of constant learning. Research without search is only a repetition. This search will enable discourse, the discourse will seek evidence, and the applied processes will deliver the evidence as a basis for a continued search.

Students now have at their disposal digital tools that allow them a whole range of creative outputs and creative possibilities. From digital drawing, 3D fabrication and film production, students can develop their ideas through speculation, making and testing in real space. But beyond the notion of technique and fabrication, students should also extend their cultural knowledge and awareness – to be receptive to the issues of society. Learning within a collaborative and cross-disciplinary environment facilitates discussion and the broadening of viewpoints.

Education should deliver the framework in which such a process can constantly unfold without limiting it through preconceived boundaries or bureaucracy. Here lies one of the main responsibilities of the educator; enabling innovative processes, placing them in measurable, verifiable frameworks to achieve clear and proven after-effects and to protect and shield these processes from preconceptions, artificial limitations and restrictions.

On the question of Format

With the ambitions of a framework that delivers applied projects through methodologies of interdisciplinary, interactive creative processes, the question of the format is inevitable. If one wants to bring together architecture, fine art, as well as socio-political topics, and deliver applied formats that create proven evidence for the arguments, then the overall format must be capable of embracing this wide field of genres. On the other hand, the format needs to be able to deliver results that are realised, tangible and comparable as well as being open to participation, experience, and critique. Performative formats in a wider definition have ranged from food, dance, music, and art to lectures and workshops and have proved themselves to be the ideal common ground for delivering frameworks of evidence.

Students should be aware of how formats are related to the concepts they are exploring and communicating. The formats are also closely related to collaboration which can enable greater complexity of space production and performance. An awareness of technology allows one to push the boundaries of format (Lorenz and Siems 2002, p 60-63). For example, the AAIS used the virtual as an innovative format during Covid. We describe the virtual teaching approach in the "Behind the Scenes" chapter within the process of delivering a life event in Seoul and Beijing whilst being in lock-down in Europe.

On the question of Design

What is in front of us is not arbitrary. It is the manifestation of the process leading to the point at which it is reviewed. This is the moment of taking stakes during events. So even though the work that takes place in an interdisciplinary environment each genre itself should be comparable to the best practice of its discrete discipline. It should not be a compromised partial approach, but rather an enriched result that enriches the knowledge and contribution of its field. This is our definition of design. Design of artefacts, design of performances as well as design of processes. None of these fields can be neglected or depend on other elements to sustain it or compensate for its shortcomings. Design is the process of bringing components together in a setting that empowers and elevates each part as well as the overall (Lorenz 2016, p 23-25).

We strive to bring an aesthetic sensibility to whatever we do, and the sense of design is an important aim within the AAIS approach. What we consider to be 'good design' is dependent on all the various facets of a project – from the harmonious, economical and elegant relations of spaces, materials, structures, choreography and orchestration of all its elements right down to details such as graphics. Design must also communicate intention.

On the question of responsibility of creativity

Our responsibility as a creator within continuously changing political and social landscapes is of most importance. None of the work we do can happen in isolation. The external factors we see around us are the reason to search for solutions, to create and to confront. As a process which from the outset is based on the negotiation of different fields, individuals and procedures, spatial performance and design offers itself as a common ground to discuss otherwise separate and contentious topics and discourses. The applied process delivers tangible outcomes that can serve as starting points that were created communally by otherwise separate or even opposing parties. The process of creating and experiencing together thus offers opportunities to think beyond one's own limits, be these set by social, political, or artistic preoccupations.

Collaborative methods within education can create an empathetic and mutualistic environment. Exchange of ideas and discussions should be encouraged as part of a creative process. Students are not only trying to find themselves as creative individuals but as individuals, who will be contributing to their community.

1.5
Foundation inhabitable
installation at Hook Park
2004. (TL)

1.6
Screenshot of the AAIS 2020 Performance
at the DSK gallery in Seoul during the covid
pandemic. (TS)

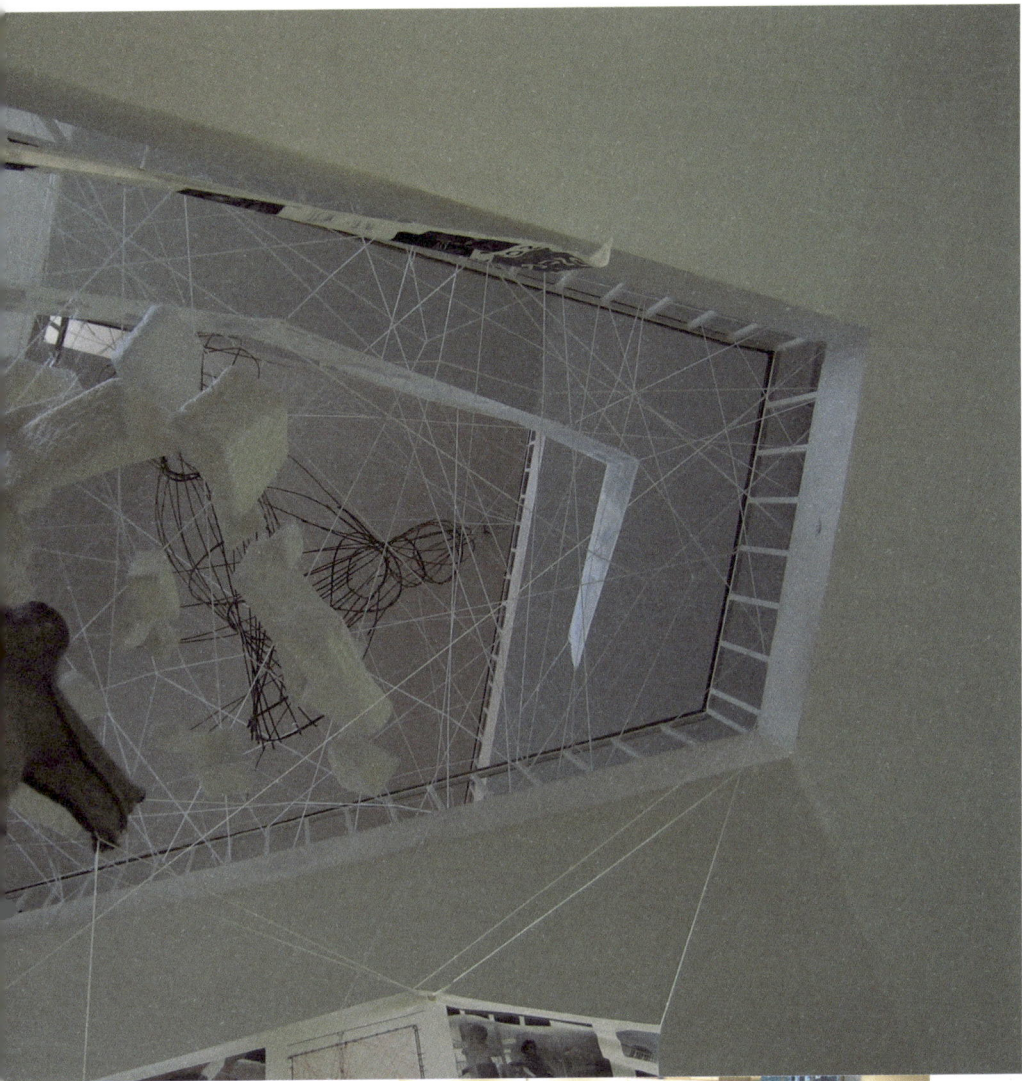

1.7
Installation of the foundation course
as part of the Tallin Architectural
Biennale in 2006. (TS)

1.8
"Settlement" Jury of Theo Lorenz's and Peter
Staub's Diploma unit 14 at the AA 2007 as
part of the Thames Gateway series. (TL)

On the question of funding in changing economic landscapes

In the creative fields the discussion about ways of support and funding is always a big question. What is the value of art, what is the value of architecture and design? This value is in most cases of creativity often limited to separate evaluations and processes that 'give value' to these fields. In the overlap of the disciplines, however, these values shift and can no longer be separated. Traditional funding means therefore often fail. The creative fields, however, seem to be one of the most dependent areas on these traditional forms of funding. Whereas, in other disciplines funding models are diversified and synergised, the arts are still relying on grants, bespoke clients and donors in predefined disciplines and areas.

With this model, art can never freely develop as it is always vulnerable to the changing economic conditions around it. The arts need economic models as procedures that allow processes to unfold regardless of an economic boom or recession. The various projects of the studio, therefore, looked at various means of production emerging from the participating initiatives and opportunities. Hatching various strategies for sustaining an economic framework for the tasks at hand, ranging from 'no budget' to in-kind and monetary support. Examples for these different ways of funding approaches are described in the "Behind the Scenes" chapter in the development of the projects in Jena, Cologne, Madrid and Logroño.

It is important that students understand the infrastructures that support a project proceeding a spatial design approach, be it in architecture, art or performance. Funding is a part of the infrastructure of a work as well as the work itself. This infrastructural support will include venues, material supply, participants, technical assistance and many more. Knowledge of this field has become vital within art and performance practice.

On the question of innovation

One of the primary goals in all creative work is innovation and the way to find it is through research, experimentation and testing. Innovation requires an understanding of the issues at hand and finding novel and economic ways of addressing them.

Finding solutions that are not just mere compromises or fixes to a problem is the constant quest of our discourse and the development of projects. This requires us to constantly seek to be 'inventors' and innovators. The resulting evidence, that proves the concept, is always a starting point for the next set of innovations. The AAIS team operates on constant innovation, based on experience and outcome.

On the question of networks and collaboration

For innovation to function, static set-ups are counterproductive. Yet constant frameworks of comparison are needed. Therefore, a combination of both systems is necessary. The format where both definitions can unify is that of collaboration within fluid networks. Each entity is definable and can take up areas of responsibility, yet in their connectivity their individual contribution has an over-transformative effect on the entities of the network. The overlaps of feedback as well as reliability and trust are the core of any functioning collaboration. In such a setting the talk in the riverside pub over a glass of wine is as important as the concentrated research and work in the separate spheres. Passion and enthusiasm, friendship and advocacy as well as enjoyment and even outrage are core motivators for exchange and collaboration. Networks in themselves require constant work and need to be proven by evidence of these basic principles to work, unfold and prosper. They cannot be sustainably created in a forced or artificial way, it needs constant nurturing and care.

In our interconnected world the ability to navigate through the creative as well as economic networks has become of growing significance. The process of negotiation of potential projects, the search and application for funding, collaboration with various stakeholders and creatives and consultants are skills that can be learned and honed. This could and should begin within an educational environment in which one can experiment with techniques and methodologies.

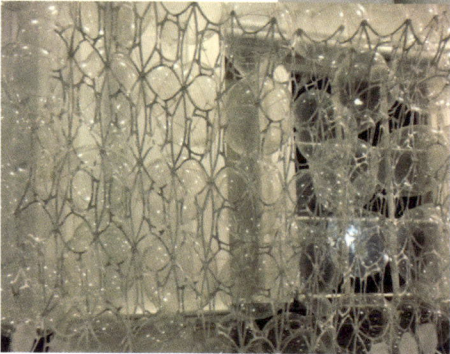

1.9
Raluca Grada in costume for the Performance
"We fight our Battles with our Drawings on the Wall"
in front of laser cut elements of the installation. (TS)

1.10
Elements of the ephemeral Balloon Towers as
part of the Performance "We fight our Battles
with our Drawings on the Wall" 2013. (TS)

Concluding paragraph

The Interprofessional Studio understands the area of Spatial Performance and Design beyond usual definitions of architecture, art and performance. It takes spatial performance as an area of spatial investigation that includes the socio-political effect of design and performance and how creative work and design acts within its given context through actual projects and applied networks in the overlap of the creative disciplines. In this way the studio forms an intense learning environment for networking within the creative fields through actual exposed and applied projects and therefore negotiated at all times. Challenging the frontiers of working in between art, architecture and performance, the AAIS aims to expose a hidden 'worknet' between multiple professions and their products.

The AAIS, as a studio-based programme, is operating as an interdisciplinary creative office. Here knowledge exchange is one of the core points of focus, reaches professions and stimulates students to develop a language with which to communicate across creative disciplines. The studio explores the creative disciplines as defined as visual art, the performing arts, design, and media practices. We recognise that such definitions are constantly evolving and the principle of the AAIS Interprofessional Studio is to challenge rather than uphold the accepted divisions of these disciplines. In today's creative professions many individuals define their work and interest as being at home in more than one discipline.

The studio gives these individuals an opportunity to step away from their existing professional or academic activities and develop new creative skills and techniques as well as enjoy the intellectual stimulation of the multidisciplinary overlap of the professions. It acts as an invitation to build a network of professionals and experts from creative backgrounds as diverse and complementary as possible, ranging from design, music, film, photography, fashion, communication, curation and performance through workshops and symposia. In this framework each combining a creative language to work and study within the AA school on concrete projects reflective of the various fields of research. Students are expected to have independence of creativity whilst having no option but to integrate into the collective practice of the ensemble. Contrary to typical interdisciplinary design approaches, where individual professions remain in their respective fields of expertise, the AAIS seeks to place its members and participants outside their comfort zone, acquiring knowledge from other disciplines that will ultimately influence, extend and adjust their own creative processes and practice.

References

Barth, Lawrence (2006) Article: Exhibitions in AA files No54, Publisher Architectural Association, London

Heidegger, Martin (1954) "Was heißt Denken?" Max Niemeyer Publisher, translated to English (1968) "What is called thinking?" Part1, Harper and Rowe publisher New York

Lorenz and Siems (2002) "Networking and Knowledge transfer through new technologies", Article in Magazine Architektur und Bauforum No221, Vienna Lorenz (2016) Article: "Design processes within creative disciplines" in the Catalogue of the Architectural Biennale Krakow

Theo Lorenz
Tanja Siems

CREATION THROUGH OUT OF THICK AIR APPROACH

We are here to create!

This is the common denominator between all the arts: the desire to turn ideas into reality. However, the question remains, what frameworks are needed to enable us to achieve our creative goals and arrive at results which are even exceeding our own expectations? The will to create is omnipresent. Seeds of initiatives are everywhere, be they small but unique or powerful yet mundane. We need to build transformative networks by finding synergies between them to enable our own creative work.

Within a globally connected environment, we can look for overlaps between initiatives and creative minds to form alliances that have multiple outcomes for participants. We no longer work out of thin air: we work within an environment pregnant with ideas. This fruitful dense atmosphere might still appear first as a thick fog, difficult to navigate and understand, with seemingly no clear boundaries nor focus. Within this confusing atmosphere of opportunities, we need to understand how to navigate in this condition. We need to learn to search for synergies and overlaps, recognise them and consolidate them to become a reliable backbone for our own creative process.

The motivation of creativity

The interesting contradiction is that what inspires us and initiates the process of creativity in the first place, be it an idea, vision, or inspiration, might become the cause of struggles, challenges, and, often enough, disappointments. All too often, we find artists being disillusioned and pessimistic about their prospects. They are waiting for external factors to change in their favour – the one big win, the one hit, the one highly rated show, the one patron, or sadly even just the one YouTube, TiKTok or Instagram post, to catapult them into the 'Hall of Fame'. Most might wait forever or see their sudden fame diminish faster than it emerged, as it lacked substance.

The key to a lasting career in the creative fields is to create an ever-growing network of collaborations and connections that allow individuals to find possibilities to unfold their potential to the fullest. We ought to ask ourselves what drives our overall ambition? Are we looking for the validation of our ideas, do we seek fame for fame's sake, or do we want to realise our ideas and be enabled to do even more creative work and opportunities to unfold these even further? These aims might not need to be entirely separated; however, they will influence how we evaluate success, seek alliances and collaborations and how open, generous and inclusive we are with our work and ideas.

There is a significant difference if seeing an idea as an *a priori* fixed aim or rather as a starting point for a process of development away and beyond it. A successful creative process should be able to arrive at a result that is at least as convincing as the initial starting point, and in the best case it exceeds our expectations.

Today, being unique requires more than simply being different or distinct from others. Being the only one of one's kind today rather means to be a transformative element within a wider assembly: able to co-create and create work outside the predictable form; able to recognise and consolidate specific and tangible outcomes within the overall work. These methodologies should form different arrangements of work relations that become the basis of successful creative careers.

Within the work of the Interprofessional Studio and beyond we try to evaluate a methodology of work that allows for creative ideas to unfold beyond pre-conceived ideas. We try to establish the circumstances that are necessary to be able to continuously realise innovative work, find one's own passion and talents and apply these within a professional environment.

We believe that in order to achieve these aims a few preconditions should be envisioned within the framework of each process: the individuals are at home in more than one discipline, they are able to be working within networks and ensembles and across multiple disciplines.

/people

We are the multitude of our talents. '/people' are networks in persona. Within this network, an internal negotiation between one's different passions and professions takes place constantly. Like external networks the '/person' needs to learn not to compromise between these different interests, but to give each of them space to unfold at the right time. Enabling each of them to the advantage of the other, and to combine them into new discipline-arching approaches in order to create work in the unique overlap of one's own talents. Each '/' should not be seen as a divider but as an integral and transformative part of one's overall professional and creative persona. Slashes here should not denote an 'or' neither an 'and', but an 'also' and 'in combination with'.

The result of these individual formula is in this way a constantly evolving and developing negotiation of dynamic and progressive factors. Thus for /people the field of occupation becomes one dynamic field of investigation across genres that is more than the sum of the defined fields. /people might still have different depth of interest and knowledge in the various areas of work; and as it is the case in external networks, each interest and discipline does not have to have the same weight and depth. Yet the multitude of interest form a field of understanding that enables us to expand our knowledge in all directions. It enables us to stay curious and add more /'s to our list of vocations as an expansive ability to move across fields of disciplines.

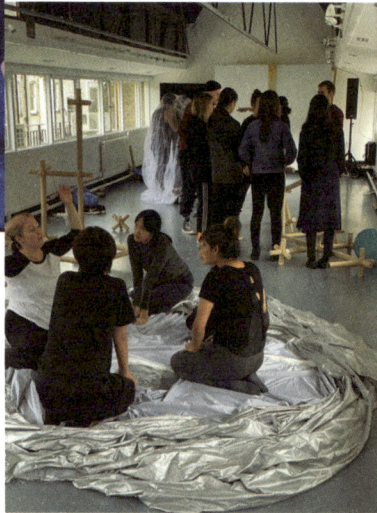

2.1
Zoie Wang performing during
the sound workshop with
Andy Dean in 2019. (TL)

2.2/3
Collaborative workshop between AAIS
and the MA/MFA in Choreography from
Trinity Laban led by Tony Thatcher. (TL)

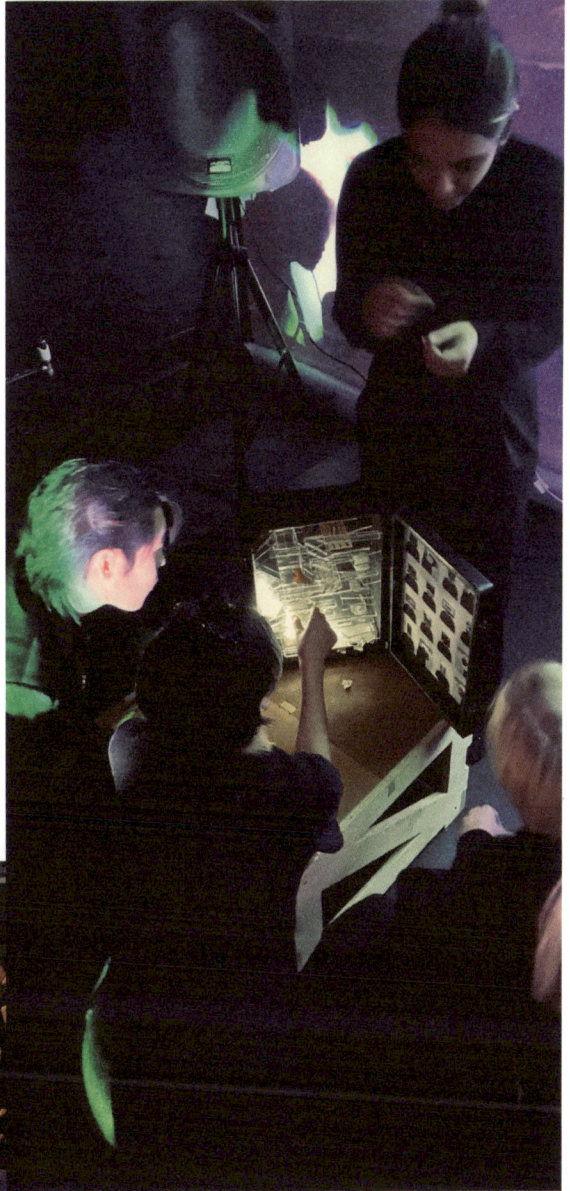

2.4
Derive workshop run
by Mona Camille and
Noa Segev 2019. (TL)

2.5
'Narrative boxes' as part of the Spatial Narrative
Workshop 2022 run by Theo Lorenz, Tanja Siems,
Vera San Payo de Lemos and Hila Shemer. (TL)

2.6
Heiko Kalmbach in discussion with
students during "Dramaturgy & Film"
Workshop 2022. (TL)

2.7
Performance "Metronome" of students
as result of the sound Workshop by Andy
Dean and David McAlmont 2022. (TL)

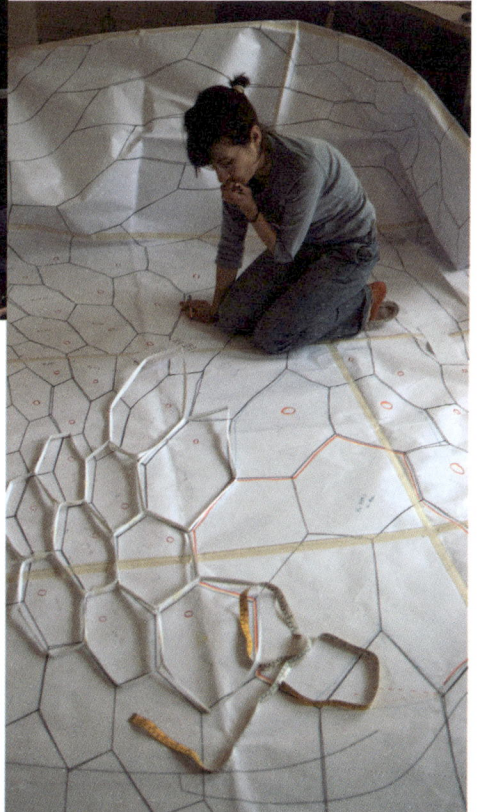

2.8
Final MFA Thesis Jury at the "Echo Festival" at the "Heal's" residency 2022. (TL)

2.9
Creative discussion of performers of New Movement Collective with Andy Dean, Theo Lorenz and Tanja Siems before the "Exquisite Corpse" performance at the Matadero Madrid in 2011. (HW)

2.10
Raluca Grada working on the "Hexa-dress" for the 2010 "Seed to Scene" festival in Covent Garden. (OG)

These negotiations will not happen in isolation. All too often one might be told to be 'all over the place' and that one should concentrate on one discipline alone to become professional. In most societies individuals are asked to specialise in one profession. These occupations become the one state of being that defines us. Often it pre-sets our standing, acceptance in society, educational path, and economic status. However, a reduction to one field of work is often a significant compromise of the interest and ambitions of the individual. In the worst case these professions do not even overlap with the core interest of the individual, merely become the occupation of most of their life. Other important parts of their interest are therefore often categorised as mere hobbies, separated distinctively from the regular job as pleasures away from work. A cross fertilisation here becomes difficult or even undesirable. This consequently would entail that work should become singular and separated from pleasure, causing one to distinguish between 'life' and 'work' and requiring us to seek a work-live balance.

In a hierarchical order separate areas of investigation might be of advantage, as task and ideas are to be executed with a depth of predefined knowledge, however without compromise or negotiation. Nonetheless as soon as we want to work on an equal basis with one another, lateral knowledge and understanding becomes fundamental.

A /person has the ideal basis to create relations and new links, both in the personal and in the professional sphere. This ability to communicate across boundaries is the basis of all connected ways of working. In the overlap of our individual fields of interests we can seek initiatives, build alliances, and create new projects. Feeling at home in more than one discipline should not be defined as neither being professional in one discipline nor another. Equally it does not mean that the /people merely work 'multiple jobs' and that this is the addition of disciplines in separation.

As an individual with one's own area of interest we can find oneself within a network of overlapping frequencies. These resulting networks are from the outset dense and expansive. Connections depend not on separate disciplines with single links to the other disciplines. They depend on a field of varied expertise with multiple overlaps to be between the fields without being fully congruent. Contrary to typical interdisciplinary design approaches, where individual professions remain in their respective fields of expertise, /people seek to place themselves outside their own comfort zone, acquiring knowledge from other disciplines that will ultimately influence, extend and adjust their own creative processes and practice. This is what we define as an 'interprofessional' approach.

An interprofessional approach relies still on a high level of specific knowledge and professionalism. However, no longer as the executing party within this field of knowledge, but rather as the teacher and mentor of this expertise to others. With such an approach the established knowledge and best practice is at all times challenged and extended by the practice and expertise of other professional fields, initiating innovation and expansion of the field itself.

Each '/' represents an opportunity for initiative, to find overlaps, and to form new connections. A wide field of interest and knowledge opens an even wider field of collaborations, especially if the person one connects to is equally a /person with overlaps with numerous differing 'slashes' within their profession. In a network of separated disciplines where a/b/c/d/e, for example an architect working with an engineer, an artist and a builder and an accountant, work together, each of them might only find a few points of direct connections. They are depending on translations of one's own profession to the other. If, however the architect is equally a practising builder, the builder is also a sculptor, the engineer is experienced in accounting and the accountant is as well working in computational architecture, the collaboration will benefit from the interprofessional experience of each member of the ensemble, its overlaps, as well as subtle differences. Communication can no longer be linear, but becomes intertwined, expanded, and enriched. The network of /people in this way become not only multidisciplinary but exponential and multidimensional.

Like a person who speaks multiple languages, it is easier to communicate across borders, create mutual understanding and create diplomatic results if one can understand in detail what is said on all sides. A discourse is not lost in translation, however enhanced by the nuances of different sensibilities of other languages. One language might still be your native tongue, yet the ability to speak and think in different languages will transform the basis of this mother tongue itself.

This multiplicity leads to new definitions of genre and work from the outset. The expanded set of skills allows for a high flexibility: how, and in what area, they might be applied or forge unique careers and alliances. When hard skills become less and less reliable, the ability to pick up new skills and create new areas of work become prime assets. Multidisciplinary artists can no longer be seen as omni-dilettantes that are neither at home in one nor the other predefined profession. When everything is at flux, a specialisation within one area bears insecurity and risk, as one is dependent on the specific skill, constantly needed in unspecific times, a machine that is waiting for the one flash to hit it as its power source.

As /people we are prone to recognise opportunities in the overlaps and similarities of the disciplines. Equally we might see shortcomings and needs for extension. Out of this position /people can actively take the initiative to create new projects and work. A project can be initiated out of individual disciplines, settings, or ideas. These initiators start to ensemble the overall collective by looking for further collaborators or other synergistic initiatives. We call this approach working 'Out of Thick Air'.

From 'A Priori' to 'Out of Thick Air'

We distinguish between four generalised approaches to design. 'a priori', moderated, 'matter of concern' and 'out of thick air'. We see the first two as less desirable and realistic within today's creative world.

A Priori – Matter of Facts

As 'a priori' design, from the outset we define an approach that sees a subjective, initial idea or design as the final aim of the overall process. The creator is working towards an individual preconceived opus. The ideas are seen as 'Matter of Facts' that therefore should not be questioned nor altered. No difference and no compromise should occur between the initial idea and its realisation and therefore the result needs to be identical with the idea. Once realised no further developments or changes are wanted, no matter how much the conditions around the creation are changing. The result is finite from start to end, a monument of the mind.

1 - "Matter of Fact"

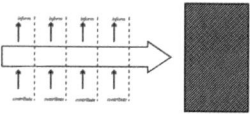

In an 'a priori' process no experiment can happen, as an experiment would require the option of an open outcome. Consequently, no discoveries, no progress and no lucky accidents or serendipities are possible within this predefined context. Change and innovation could only happen purely in the mind as part of the initial idea.

This linear approach leaves no space for negotiation and only seeks collaboration and contribution to help and sustain a fixed idea. Any diversion or negotiation is considered a limitation and compromise to the original idea. This way of working requires working conditions that are ideal to entirely serve the starting idea. It, therefore, requires calculable and predefined means of procurement from the start to end of the process and avoid any shifts in conditions that lead to a diminished result: The creator and any contributor has the talent and ability to translate the idea into reality, the materials, techniques and external conditions for the creation exist and customers and supporters of the project are dedicated and reliable throughout. In such a condition the architect needs a 'dream client', that follows all the ideas and provides all necessary budget; the musician requires a perfect record contract with a powerful label that still takes no influence on the creative process; and the artist has a gallery and list of collectors that provides security and a high level of exposure at all times.

We all know that this is a situation that is not realistic. However, the idea of a 'pure' creative process is still a main driver behind many creative ambitions and therefore a main cause of disappointment if it is not achieved. Artists and creators of all kinds are still evaluated on the ability to create their work without compromise.

Compromise – Matters of Moderation

The reality of most, if not all, creation processes lead to a moderated approach. The work changes over time due to various external influences. Changing circumstances of collaboration, clients, financial or material conditions influence the realisation of the initial idea over time. The difference lies within the starting attitude towards these matters of moderation. Are changes welcome to achieve an overall better result within the given task, or are they seen as compromising the initial goal? Within an 'a priori' premiss the process of moderation is seen as leading to unwanted diversion from the original idea. A lot of energy and effort is spent to keep these diversions as limited as possible or to avoid them all together and to keep the process 'on course'. The moderation in this case is focused on limitation, rather than alteration. All development is a narrow, inward-looking process towards a fixed target. Therefore, alternatives and evolutions are not given the space and possibility to develop, leading to a result that in comparison to the original idea is evaluated as less than the starting point and a compromise. The success of the moderation is seen as how close the result is to the 'ideal' outcome.

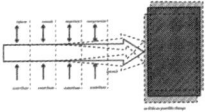

"Matter of Fact" - Moderated

If changes are anticipated from the outset the process of moderation might lead to an enriched and expanded result overall. The concentration would focus on achieving the best result of the envisioned idea with the help of the given circumstances, rather than contempt them. The focus of the moderation process would be on achieving the predefined goal within a wider framework.

Matter of Concerns – Design of the Design Process

In a further step we might not only anticipate and moderate changes within a design process but seeing them as an integral part of the work itself. Within an approach that considers all 'matters of concern' of an idea, a term coined by Bruno Latour (2004), every step towards a final outcome is considered a necessary point of negotiation and readjustment. The initial idea is no longer seen as an indisputable and unchangeable fact, but rather as the initiator of a process, that expects from the outset that the result will be different and enriched in comparison to the first idea. This way of working invites the integration of wide networks of thought and applies them into a process driven development of the ideas, the progression of the work here becomes a creative task in itself: the design of the design process (Lorenz 2013).

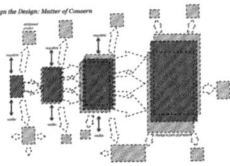

Design the Design: Matter of Concern

Every in-between result of the process becomes a project in its own right triggering the next forward development of the overall project towards a wider defined aim. Detours and variations are anticipated and welcome. In this context negotiation does not lead to compromise but to a positive readjustment of the project in relation to its actual concerns. With this framework a project can be evaluated along its way and understood as a definable outcome. The project is no longer either completed or unfinished, it is all times existing and nascent. In this way the project at hand can stop before the outcome is achieved, yet the 'in-between' result can be seen as a fully-fledged project. Crucially a design of the design process results in a multitude of outcomes on the path towards the overall initiating goal. Each point of revaluation becomes a moment of realisation, resulting in either a detour of the next step or a bifurcation or multiplication of realisations. For example, the drawing of the initial idea of a building might lead to an exhibition that displays it in a wider context to an audience, the exhibition in turn might lead to the creation of an additional venue and a publication, that might lead to new collaborations and partners. All in-between results are additional creative results supporting the overall process and negotiation of the original idea. Even if the process would stop at any point, it would have actual applied realisations. The outcome, also the original goal was never reached, would have numerous results rather than a singular 'all or nothing' termination.

Undoubtedly, this way of working requires much higher attentiveness from all participants. All parts of the collective have to be in a constant dialogue and the work has to be at all times ready for evaluation, and visible to allow for forward negotiation. However, the creative energy is spent on actual tangible results at the here and now rather than to maintain hypothetical futures. Within such a framework of matters of concerns, the overall ambition might still be driven by the definition of an envisioned aim. The overall process still depends on linear path within a predefined framework, even if the process is open, allows to bifurcate and detour from the path. Without the preconceived idea, the process might not start in the first place.

Out of Thick Air

In a further step, we try to replace these overall aims with a wider definition of synergies between different initiatives. In such an 'Out of Thick Air' approach, various existing initiatives and interests are hedged together to initiate the work progress. Within the overlap of these initiatives new synergistic projects emerge. Genre, size, duration, and budget become variables within a larger dynamic network that aspires to create a multitude of outcomes. The synergistic overlap leads to one or more overall projects of otherwise discreet initiatives that are in combination more than the sum of them all.

An important aspect of this way of working is the equality of initiatives in terms of ambition and intensity. An initiative that, for example, aims at publishing a spatial photo series might look for designer, architects, dancers, and costume designers, whereas it would be less in need of music. Obviously, within this subset, the dancers, for example, would need a sonic environment to perform and create a feasible piece of work, and would hence extend the network to musicians. The different ambitions create additional, overlapping networks, and leads to new creations. This would challenge original initiatives to extend their approach and create new forms of work or multiple synchronous results. In an ideal case the new connections establish new initiatives and formations in turn.

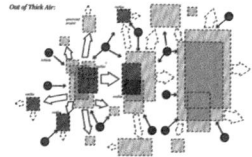

In an 'Out of Thick Air' approach the 'scanning' for initiatives becomes the main skill. The starting point here is no longer a fully developed project idea, but rather fields of interests and ambitions that drive the search for complementary partners and connections. Once a field of overlap of interest is discovered further ideas can be developed forward in multiple directions. It is a constant exchange of analysis and production and therefore becomes the foundation of all work from the beginning.

Virtuous work bears the same attitude within its process as within its results: from the search for initiatives and the definition of your network to the design, all the way to production of products of this design. Along the way, the work undulates between precise scanning and redefining. Within such a setting the results will always be accurate, yet welcoming for further development, opening many pathways for all its components, both its human participants but as well the created artefacts, physical or virtual.

All projects of the AAIS collective are following this process of scanning for initiatives. The studio formulates each year a wider field of interest and investigations. With these topics in mind the search for overlapping alliances brings together a series of potential partners of individuals and institutions that start to formulate shared, but as well separate, aims and ambitions. The studio with its group of students from various backgrounds will now start to develop synergistic propositions within the overlap of the overall network. The form, shape, extension and outcome of the overall project is not predefined. However, based on evidence of previous interventions, the overall format, quality and intensity of each project can be anticipated and envisioned. The trust of the partners is not based on a promised, predefined outcome, it is rather based on a proven track record of delivering unique and bespoke development of work as the result of the collaboration.

The studio's first collaboration with the Matadero Madrid "Exquisite Corpse" in 2011 (AAIS, 2011) can be described as a good example of a process that started 'Out of Thick Air', still resonating today. The studio's interest in staging a genre-defying event with its students from various disciplines intersected here with the ambition of the group of young choreographers and performers of "New Movement Collective (NMC)" to stage an international performance to bring the entire team together. At the same time the Matadero Madrid aimed to open its new cultural centre, whilst still many areas of development were still under process. Each of the initiatives by themselves would have had difficulties to reach their aim independently. Yet, in the overlap the shortcomings of one partner might have been the strength of the other. Whereas the risk of an unfinished site, with a shifting timeline, might have been too big a risk for a traditional production company, the flexible setting allowed the AAIS group to experiment in different and multiple ways, with events, workshops, and smaller interventions at the same time. Yet the partnership with NMC allowed from the outset to develop one visible and professional performance as the core of the network of events. For all partners these initiating events lead to several continued collaborations, as a group and individually, that exponentially unfolded in unexpected areas of works, such as culinary, political, and cultural projects over the coming years.

The process of working in a 'Out of Thick Air' modus is not a homogeneous process that follows each time the same development. Each initiative has its own starting points, dynamics, and reactions. The basis of all processes, therefore, is an attitude that is actively looking for possibilities of collaboration with an open mind, not expecting others to act first or bringing predefined areas to the projects. A few general conditions, however, can be drawn out to demonstrate recognisable patterns. These patterns often overlap and combine in multiple ways.

a Priori - "Matter of Fact"

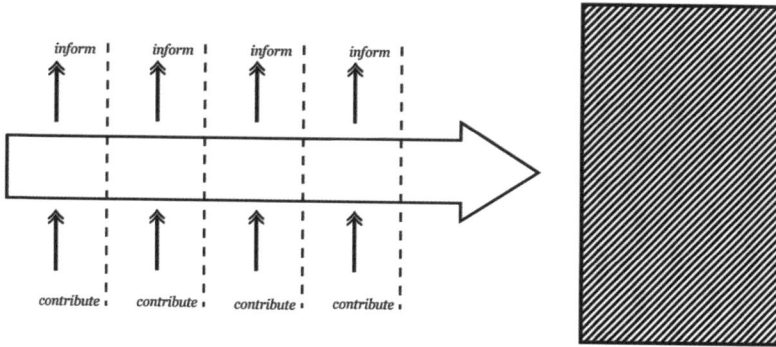

"Matter of Fact" - Moderated

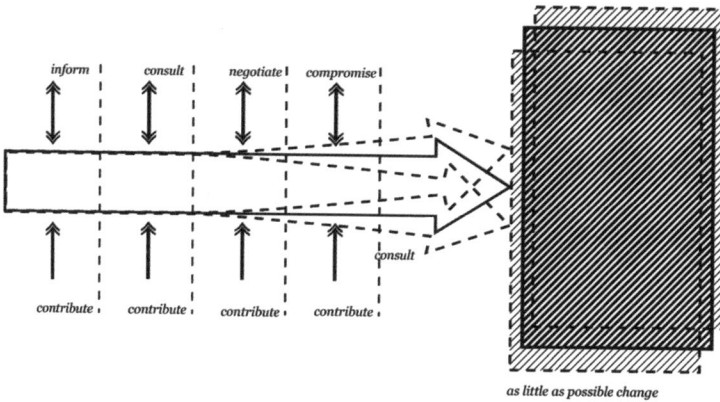

as little as possible change

2.11
Diagram of an "A priori" approach, where the initial idea should be executed without compromise or negotiation. (TL)

2.12
Diagram of the moderated a priori approach, where result is diverting the initial aim. (TL)

Design the Design: Matter of Concern

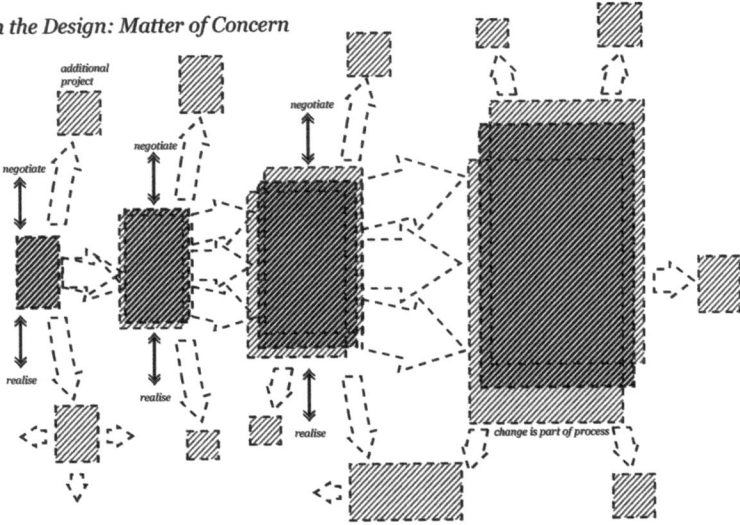

Out of Thick Air:

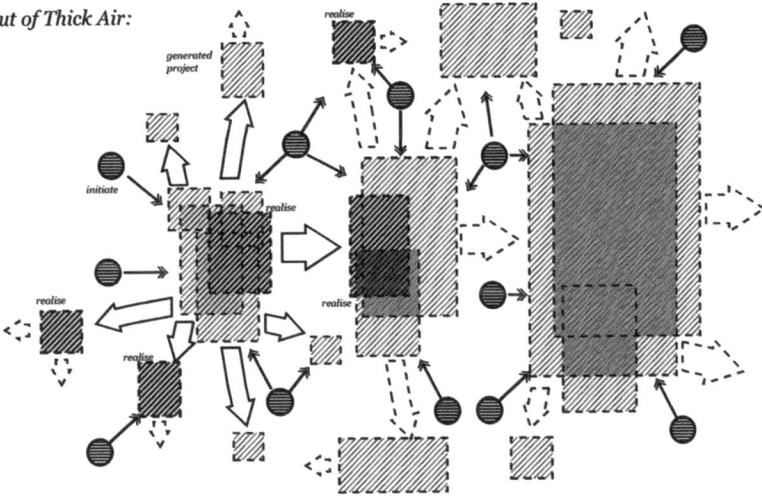

2.13
Diagram of a "Design of the Design" Process,
where each step is seen as a fully realised project,
initiating the next iteration and bifurcations. (TL)

2.14
Diagram of the "Out of Thick Air" approach, where the starting point of any
given project is based does no longer require a fixed starting point or final aim
but is initiated by overlapping initiatives of any given size or discipline. (TL)

Projects within established frameworks or grants

Within the arts a setting where projects are developed based on topics that relate to established frameworks or grants is common. These could be applications to funds for circular festivals or exhibitions such as biennials or triennials or grant applications for anniversaries of important cultural events. In both cases the initiatives have to develop ideas within a given set of aims and organisational structures. This means that the initiative is limited in scope and extent to these frameworks. However, these limitations are often compensated by a larger reach of the project, allowing for a higher exposure of the project, and allowing to establish new connections. The external framework becomes the main hub for networks and thus the initiative is taken towards this project.

The studio has been part of several such established frameworks, ranging from the "Bauhaus Lab" in Jena, the "Architectural Triennale" in Lisbon, the "ReSet" Celebration in Barcelona and the Concéntrico Festival in Logroño. Each of them building important connections for the AAIS studio because of a strong collaboration within the project and the leading institution. The "Bauhaus Lab", as part of an EU Cultural Programme, Education and Culture DG (Holt and Schäfer 2009), enabled the AAIS studio to realise its first initiating year as a multifaceted and diverse programme. The funding allowed for professional collaboration as a full-organisational Partnership between the Theatre Jena, the AA Emtech programme, the Centre for Culture and Communication C3 in Budapest, the Art and Educational Centre EMAHO in Marseille, the E-Werk event centre in Weimar, the Department of Cultural Affairs of the City of Weimar, Webb Yates Engineers and Inflate London to take place. At the same time given the strict framework of an EU grant the preparation time, organisation and final reporting extended over several years. For projects of this scale the advantages for the network and project needs to be always weighed against the organisational effort that needs to be taken. Are the lasting effects worth the effort or do the limitations of the project prohibit lasting effects to unfold?

The organisational burden is much reduced if the project is invited to the established framework but is not part of the overall organisational framework. This was case for both the Lisbon Triennale project as well as the Concéntrico project in Logroño. In both cases the studio was a guest of the overall organisation. Whereas this reduces the overall organisational burdens and risks, it requires the project to respond to a brief developed by the partners. The new networks one can establish on this basis are those between the host and the studio, but as well towards the other guests of the organisation. However, quite rightfully the biggest after-effect and feedback will be established for the framework organisation and host, and thus the reach of the individual project might be limited.

Projects hosted within a specific local or political setting
A different framework might be if the project is hosted by an individual institution
or location without a strict overall curatorial framework. Here, the project is coming
to this location to initiate new possibilities and generate tangible after-effects
for both the studio and the partners. These collaborations are often a good
starting point if we can recognise a need for testing of new ideas and concepts
or a need for negotiation or finding consent in relation to the partnering host. In
these cases, the project becomes a mediator of ideas. The project series at the
Matadero Madrid and the projects in the DQE centre in Cologne, at "Las Heras"
in Girona, the "New Museum" in Beijing and the "Teatro Abierto" in Lisbon can be
categorised in such a way. The studio was able to unfold in all these distinctive
settings projects within their own set of aims, however responding to the needs
of the hosting partners. In such settings the events are besides performances
often contextualised as a wider field of activities that bring audiences together,
such as workshops, culinary events, and talks.

Projects as host
The dynamic of the initiative is changing direction if the studio itself becomes
the inviting host. Here the prime starting point relies on the studio itself as the
organiser of the festival and event. The overall dynamic of such a project is of
actively bringing in new partners and artists towards the project of the studio.
This way of working helps to establish new partnerships and test new areas of
investigations with experienced artists from different genres. Especially, the
"Seed to Scene" festival in London's cultural quarter Covent Garden has been
such an event. Besides initiating new working relations with music through Andy
Dean and David McAlmont as well as dance and choreography through New
Movement Collective and the scientist Wolfgang Stuppy (Kesseler and Stuppy
2006), the festival was 'seeding' a series of political, organisational, and strategic
alliances for the studio. In such a setting, however, the overall starting risk, with
the organisation of the support, construction, security etc. rests entirely with the
producing studio.

2.15
Inflatable canopy at the Theaterhaus
Jena as part of the "Bauhaus Lab"
2009 project. (TL)

2.16
The Cloud during the performance "Flow
Fields" with New Movement Collective
during the Lisbon Triennale 2013. (VB)

2.17
Andi Hu performing during "The Walk"
in Logroño in Spain as part of the
4th Concéntrico festival in 2018. (TS)

2.18
Performance "Trust, Truth, Integrity"
at the Las Heras venue in Girona with
New Movement Collective in 2017. (VB)

2.19
Culinary event as part of
the "Trust, Truth, Integrity"
festival at Las Heras. (VB)

2.20/21/22
Xiu Ran and Xi Cheng performing
in AAIS Performance "Origin" at the
Yue-Art Museum at Beijing. (TZ)

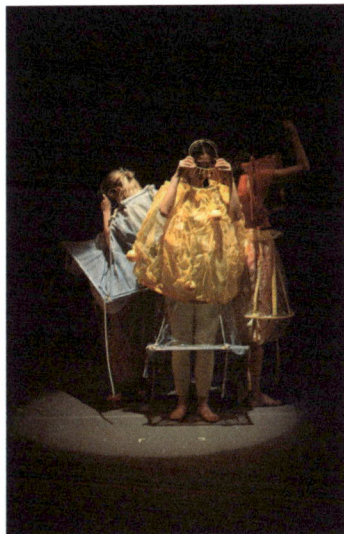

2.23
Ina performing in the "Seen"
Performance as part of the AAIS
"Moult" festival at the Teatro
Aberto in Lisbon in 2023. (AR)

2.24
"Partida" Performance as part
of the AAIS "moult" festival at
the Teatro Aberto in Lisbon in
2023. (AR)

2.25
"Parding your Beggon"
Performance as part of the AAIS
"moult" festival at the Teatro
Aberto in Lisbon in 2023. (AR)

2.26
"Metamorph" Performance
as part of the AAIS "moult"
festival at the Teatro Aberto
in Lisbon in 2023. (AR)

Projects of overlapping frequencies

In a project of overlapping frequencies these burdens are shared by a series of co-operating partners. Each partner covers parts of the overall framework in such a way that in the overlap of all co-organisers the artistic and organisational aspects of the festival are covered. In an ideal case all aspects of the other forms of initiatives mentioned before are taking place embedded into this network of shared responsibilities and successes. A good example of this approach is the "Spatial Performance Festival" in Athens. In an overlap of the different artist of the studio, such as GesamtAtelier and David McAlmont in overlap with our students and partners, a festival was formed that featured multiple performances over a period of a week. Each project was contextualised and enhanced by each other, whilst still maintaining their independence.

A feasible approach to creativity

Such a creative process can only be successful if it is feasible in artistic, technical and economic terms. One of the first questions that almost any creative work has to defend is how it makes economic sense. This seems to be the case, independent from the overall economic or political situation. Culture and the arts notoriously seem to have one of the least reliable frameworks. In times of economic hardship, funds for the arts are often the first ones to be cut. With political change we can all too often see a shift in cultural perspective or even restrictions. On the other end of the spectrum, in times of economic and political stability, opportunities for small artistic ventures might be limited by difficulties of competing with larger, established organisations and more often even the lack of affordable resources such as space and equipment. Rather than being caught between a rock and a hard place, we believe the arts' potential lies precisely in this apparent contradiction. The main ingredient for success today is being able to navigate complex situations. To achieve their aims artists and other creatives need to forge alliances at all times, and thus in a way become a stable factor of connectivity between other entities at flux. With this we believe the most important skills the creative individual needs are the abilities to recognise overlaps, create connections, to frame synergies and to develop lasting after-effects as a result. In this view, a creative is the quintessential entrepreneur.

In opposite to many other areas of the economy, where flexible models and the ability for fast adaptation seems to be anticipated from the outset, somehow, within the creative arts, a flexible way of thinking and adaptation, however, seems to be still dismissed. Interestingly, however, cultural projects have a high potential to provide a mediating area of activity far beyond its own realm.

Through culture and cultural exchange, as a mediator, a common ground between otherwise contrasting parties can often easily be achieved than by other initiatives mainly driven by economy, politics, or social issues. Precisely here lies the potential of the creative disciplines. In the overlap of otherwise distant activities, creative collectives and creatives can forge alliances that have a synergistic effect on all involved parties. This can happen in multiple scales and in formations between otherwise distant or unrelated entities. Art in all its different forms can create links between cities and its citizens, competing companies, institutions and organisations, subjects, and objects. Culture and creativity as the active and linking element becomes a necessary entity. It is the constant in changing times and in turn feeds and grows on these different influences and is constantly enriched through it, no matter the situation.

Beyond the pure financial consideration, the economic base of a creative occupation is to be seen in a much broader sense. For most artists, be it architects, choreographers, fine artists or fashion designers the day is not divided into a nine-to-five job and spare time. Life is rather a continuous transition between work and leisure. In this, artists might become a prototype of work in societies where 'workplaces' are no longer easy to define as clear professions or in 35- or 40-hour weeks. Job descriptions are continuously evolving or even disappearing. Artists already, if they like it or not, continuously re-evaluate their work, its framework, and its feasibility as well as their life quality. With a growing number of established jobs becoming replaceable by robots and 'AI' these 'post-digital' soft skills and adaptability also become more and more necessary within other occupations. Creatives here have already a clear economical edge.

Being able to act within various networks of collaboration is a vital ingredient for any competitive business. Social skills and the ability to recognise strength and weakness within oneself, as well as others, to be able to form alliances; these are key necessities for successful entrepreneurs and leaders alike.

If one is at home in more than one discipline it is unlikely one would be comfortable to work within strict hierarchical systems, as it would be hard to establish which disciplines would be on what level in the hierarchy in a constant manner. An ensemble of /people therefore are more likely to follow a dynamic, flat hierarchy with changing areas of responsibilities in overlap. Initiative, inventiveness, and flexible thinking are here the main linking tasks.

In hierarchical structures of the past, a favoured test for potential employees was to ask the candidate to drive the boss to the next meeting. The purpose of this stealth interview test was to determine the confidence of the driver, his reaction under stress or in unforeseen situations. How he reacted to instruction – within or against the given set of rules. This kind of test makes sense if the prospective candidate is supposed to work within a given set of standards and hierarchy. Without streets, clear destination, traffic laws and other traffic participants, this test would make less sense, especially in relation to potential collaboration.

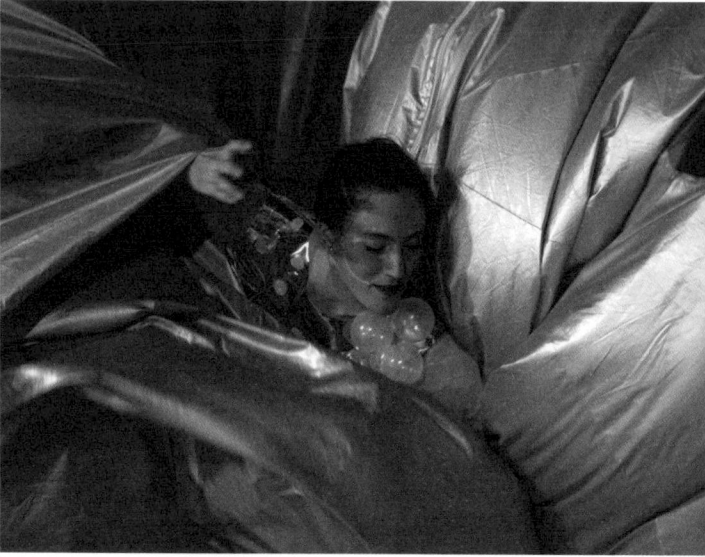

2.27/28/29/30/31
"Spatial Performance Festival" at
the Romantso in Athens (AL)

To see if creative and collaborative aspects of potential collaborators work, another test seems to be more meaningful: Preparing a meal together. In difference to driving, here candidates should use inventive, social and combinational skills from the outset. The old proverb 'too many cooks spoil the broth' assumes that too many people working on the same task will create a mediocre result. The problem here lies within the singular definition of the aim, a single soup or broth rather than a menu that results in an overall balanced and complementing set of dishes.

To create such a menu, one should be able to work with the given ingredients or have the means to organise them, be able to anticipate or discuss the likes and dislikes of the others, respond to other ideas and dishes, organise work-flow, take up specific tasks and responsibilities and create together a meal that is at least satisfying, or, in the best case, beyond expectations. The entire first actual collaboration leads to an actual event, the meal. The event itself was foreseeable as a framework yet not in all its details. In this way, the first collaboration with its conversations during the meal can lead to further discussions and interactions.

Can we work together?

A form of collaboration that looks for temporary alliances is quite common among young creatives, to enable them to create work. However, these connections are often seen as necessities rather than real opportunities of innovation.

The shared product of the collaboration should not be seen as the finite art piece but as a foundation to individual creative ideas. A good basis will allow for a much higher individual outcome: how far each individual goes, far and beyond, is up to them. But a group of ambitious co-creators will always inspire each other to go further and further. A good, experienced individual should be able to collaborate on the highest level to achieve even more ambitious aims, whilst the less experienced should be able to learn and equally contribute to the overall creation.

The collaboration is the starting point not a finite goal. Even if no fully developed project exists at the outset, each individual will have predefined ideas. Within such a process of negotiation, this is not only expected but essential. Without defined positions as a tangible starting point no discussion, no negotiation, and consequently, no outcomes are possible. The important difference here is that these ideas and positions are not seen as preconditions but as elements of the process that need to be analysed in detail, within the overall settings of all other components. Through these analyses it should be possible to formulate the essence of each idea. Once the true purpose of each component is recognised, it is easier to see synergy and overlaps between all ideas and parts, and thus to readjust and transform the overall process and design at every step.

The ability to collaborate and thrive within a group environment varies succinctly with different individuals: No group of collaborators is ever the same. This leads to the conclusion that there can't be a single recipe to harmonise all workforces. Instead, the aim would be to create frameworks and support networks that allow for a variety of dynamics and direct these differences at the same time towards a productive, creative environment. Additionally, almost no group constantly has the same dynamic in itself. The way of working can change and undulate dramatically over the course of a collaboration. The importance here is to be able to understand the dynamic in its flow and help to constantly shape and reshape it. Organisation becomes an act of choreography.

Even though the overall dynamic of collaboration might never be identical, certain patterns are reoccurring and can be defined as such. Most of us, be it tutor, student or professional, can relate to more than one of these patterns if not permanently, at least from time to time, and therefore it is helpful to be aware and utilise these patterns in a constructive way.

Working within creative networks takes some getting used to; often this is due to a top-down structure within artists' education or practice. Surprisingly, this seems to be still particularly present within the fine arts. Despite the emergence of more and more artist 'collectives' a lot of today's artistic work still seems to follow a hierarchical structure. One studies 'under' a renowned artist in a 'Master' class or is an artist with a specific gallery. With this mind-set individuals are in search for an environment that serves this fixed defined aim. Coming from such an environment the aim all too often, even if subconscious, is to become the next 'Master' and escalate within the perceived hierarchy. Thus, these artists are in the market for individual fame, becoming the next big 'star'-artist or -architect, -designer, -filmmaker, you name it. Most of the 'famous' artists seek to emulate, having extensive networks to source from, both horizontally and vertically. Isolated geniuses rarely exist. If the networks are not artistic there are other networks of support, be it curators, monetary support, critics, that enable them to be the artists they are. Many artists try to get the attention of these networks individually, an unlikely chance. Alternatively, and more sustainably, own networks should be built over time in a sustainable collective.

At the beginning of a collaboration, many young artists come with the preoccupation of having to create their own outstanding piece of art. Being different to all other artists is one of the main tasks. Collaboration is only seen to aid one's own work. This is signified by the importance of 'solo exhibitions' or 'solo concerts' in relation to 'group shows'. You are only exhibiting or performing amongst others as long as you have not gained enough fame to earn your own solo show. What is missing in this approach is that in the pursuance of uniqueness an artist must be capable of embracing as many ideas as possible. To achieve this at a young age, with little live experience and hopefully little crisis, sharing and building experience with others is recommended. The individual opus here can be found not merely in a separated piece of work but by zooming into an overall ensemble. It is not a coincidence that many artists known today have been part of a wider school of thought and movement throughout their career, excelling within those contexts, rather than by separation from them.

Even if everyone within an ensemble realises that individual success is best reached outside a fixed hierarchy, every group has to some extent individuals that drive the project. At best these 'drivers' are different individuals over the process of the project or multiple of these characters run in parallel to others to push the entire project forward together. This can only happen if these 'drivers' are at the same time motivators, able to take the group with them, trigger the ambitions of others and allow others to take over. Otherwise, the collective would end up again in a hierarchical order only arriving at the aim of a single driver rather than beyond. Ambition is important within a team. It leads to a healthy competition that brings the project forward. With a group of equally ambitious participants an outcome that would only be the smallest possible denominator would be unacceptable. Compromise, even, if necessary, in intermediate steps, is unacceptable for the overall result. Instead, over time, such a group would always thrive for negotiations that embrace all individuals' aspirations and form projects that are more than the mere addition of components.

If individuals feel that they have to compromise too much they need to either raise their own ambitions or readjust their means of negotiation by reassessing their own abilities. In each group, alliances are formed. In ideal cases these are strategic and are changing over time in relation to the tasks at hand. In less ideal cases these cause tensions or splits within the group. The key to success is to strategically learn when to continue to collaborate, despite tensions, to gain as much knowledge and experience precisely from these frictions and when to bifurcate in an informed manner. Obviously, not everybody has to be able to continuously collaborate. However, everyone can learn from one another and recognise what kind of collaborators and forms of co-creation work best in each given situation.

In successful projects reciprocal relations with others continue, rather than abrupt splits. Even if no direct collaboration might happen in the future, extended networks based on shared experience are important investments in the future. The resulting 'chosen' networks for future collaborations benefit from the overlaps of the extended network of experience.

Splits and conflict often emerge through unsubstantiated critique. Critique is easy; creation is difficult. Yet one can't function without the other. The balance between the two is what makes the important difference. Within a team, we can often observe a tendency that critique is used to bring one's own idea forward or to hide one's own weaknesses, rather than to enhance the overall progress of the team. A 'constructive' criticism all too often turns into a complaint against something. The question with critique is always its intent. An actual constructive criticism within a collaborative environment should be accompanied with a proposition that contributes to a solution of the critiqued entity within its wider field of concerns. If this is not the case all too often critique might lead to a call for order and even hierarchy. A sense of chaos is often perceived at those moments where individuals feel things not going their specific way. In this moment, the call for a higher instance comes into play. Often here we can exchange 'you should tell...' with 'I want!'.

However, collaboration should in the best cases expand the knowledge of each participant throughout the team. This is true on all levels of the network, from the teachers or group leaders to students and volunteers. If the collaboration merely ends up with a predicable pre-conceived idea, it is fair to assume that little learning and innovation has occurred. The result of such pre-conceived results might still be professional and of a high standard, but most likely would have followed a routine rather than advance multiple possibilities and new ideas. Co-learning is the main advantage of collaboration. An open mind to new and sometimes very different ideas is the key to expand one's own knowledge beyond known best practice.

The opposite of the 'stubborn approach' is passivity. Equally, this approach will not lead to innovation and learning. Passive 'soldiers' don't question the brief, the given ideas, and tasks, rather they are looking for the right or 'pleasing' answer, the path of least resistance. This again might lead to professional, yet predictable results. The teamwork might seem easy and friction free, but innovation remains minimal. Collaborators turn into employees not entrepreneurs. Often team members with 'stubborn fixed ideas' try collaborating with 'passive soldiers' resulting in projects that provided little possibilities of learning for either and might have worked better in a classical hierarchical environment than within flat hierarchies. A missed opportunity.

How we work together
A key advantage of working within an environment of a range of disciplines creates an opportunity of innovating one's own field of professional knowledge. Various forms of collaborations across disciplines are known and established. Even though the distinctions seem often quite minimal, they have a substantial influence on the mind-set and strategy within the teams. The most general terms, interdisciplinary and multidisciplinary, mostly refer to work consisting out of more than one discipline collaboration in an overall team within their own field of expertise alongside the others. Each team member relies on the work and expertise of the others to create an overall outcome.

Within transdisciplinary work, a higher degree of exchange and co-learning should occur so that the ideas and approaches of other fields of research and work can be applied within a final result. Nevertheless, each participant often remains within their own field of expertise. When we talk about interprofessional work, however, we try to go one step further. The expert here should no longer execute himself the work of the respective discipline but rather become the point of reference and tutor for his peers within the team who will bring their own knowledge and reinterpretation to the task. In this way, every team member becomes tutor and student at the same time. Everyone works out of their own comfort zone and thus brings new ideas and sensibilities to the tasks at hand and must apply them professionally. In such an environment, every professional continues to learn new skills outside the respective discipline but, even more importantly, within the discipline due to the unusual and new feedback received.

This way of working requires each team member to constantly take responsibility for specific areas of knowledge, as well as applied tasks. These responsibilities vary succinctly and often include tasks that seem less creative. However, they are essential to the success of the overall project. Responsibility and execution of work here is not necessarily the same. On the one hand, it seems merely to be the point of reference for a specific area of knowledge, making sure that professional and artistic standards within the respective fields are met. On the other hand, it implies responsibly executing tasks that might lie outside your areas of expertise. All team members must be able to rely on each other and be interdependent when it comes to defined areas of responsibility.

A team that is able to rely on each other is in need of a seamless and fluid communication. In an international, multi-disciplinary, -cultural and -generational environment it is a mistake to think that communication can happen on an even level from the outset. It has proven most successful over the years to fully embrace the differences whilst creating in each team, anew, a strategy of exchange allowing for each member of the collective to equally use their best means of communication. The catalysts for difference are the applied projects; shared common tasks, like an event that has to happen on a specific day for a specific audience, forms the necessary framework for communication to happen. The differences of the starting point here will become the ingredient that makes the outcome specific and unique.

A big part of collaboration comes down to trust. As soon as we don't know something we need to rely on the knowledge of others. We need to trust that this knowledge is correct and to the level we expect it to be. At the same time, we ourselves need to be trusted. This is the basis of collaboration. To build said trust, a team needs to gather the experience of each other's abilities and ways of working. In an environment where the work is constantly looping between realisation and development this evidence is built over time. This requires a high level of commitment and willingness to expose one's abilities through actual results. The applied nature of the work requires constant testing and realisation of ideas. Hesitation, dwelling on individual challenges, or endless discussions only delay the production of evidence that can be evaluated and tested by the team in its entirety.

Only matters that are evident can be analysed, transformed and brought forward to the next level of development evaluated by the team. Waiting for consent on every task before producing evidence will slow down the evolution of the ideas and in turn diminish an overall agreement as a consequence; the difference lies within the attitude of production. The produced outcomes are not there to be the precious, fixed outcomes, but offer themselves as a starting point of negotiation. The more evidence is produced, the faster progress will happen. The realities and pressure of the actual applied project will give rhythm to the process.

Evidence of work becomes all the more important in relation of the core team to extended partners and supporters. Most new partners, sponsors or clients wish to see a track record of work that guarantees a quality of outcome. Innovative work by default cannot easily show evidence of known entities and hence needs to be able to demonstrate a reliable framework that produces evaluable elements of development in accordance with the discussed aims. In case of the Interprofessional Studio, the evidence can be shown again in different scales and formations: the overall reputation of the Architectural Association; case stories of the studio's work over the years; biographies and the standing of its tutors, partners and alumni in practices; and the growing, applied and actual work of the new team of students at work on the current task. In a similar way, almost all teams can construct these layers of evidence, and what elements are highlighted in what way depends on the potential partner. In the overlap of all evidence the points of synergy and mutual benefit for new partners should become visible.

Conclusion

Working 'Out of Thick Air' is not something one can just instantly jump to and apply. In its components it is nothing unusual or new. The methodology rather requires us to slowly adjust our attitude to our own work. It is a process of constant evaluation, learning and application. Even after 17 years of the Interprofessional Studio as an example of this way of networked collaboration, we constantly evolve as a team, re-adjust and learn. We can witness how all parts of the process bifurcate in the careers of our alumni and change the work of all members of the network to new interesting ventures. The entire growing network keeps on adjusting to each new situation and environments proven by evidence of production. As long as this happens the network is alive and active and can serve as an example for many like-minded individuals and groups. /

References
Holt, Magdalena and Schäfer, Kathrin (2009) "Bauhaus Lab": An international network of interdisciplinary laboratories, EU Culture Programme Report
Kesseler, Rob and Stuppy, Wolfgang (2006) with Papadakis, Alexandra (Editor) "Seeds: Time Capsules of Life", London
Latour, Bruno (2004) Article: Why Has Critique Run out of Steam? From Matters of Fact to Matters of Concern
Lorenz, Theo (2013) Article: "Design of the Design Process" in Mediating Architecture, Theo Lorenz, Peter Staub, Bedford Press, London
Project AAIS 2010-11, Event series 'Exquisite Corpse' in Cologne, London and Madrid with Amaya Ducuru Clothier, Diego Ulrich, Henrietta Williams, May Safwat, Nazili Usta, Architectural Association School of Architecture (AA), London

3

Albena Yaneva
Theo Lorenz
Tanja Siems

THE NETWORKED STUDIO: AGENCY AND INTERPROFESSIONAL COLLABORATIONS

Agency and Interprofessional Collaborations

Architectural education is constantly reformed by architectural associations and registration boards around the world with the aim to help architects prepare for the organisational, economic, and managerial realities of a world that keeps moving at a greater pace. The crisis in thinking about architectural education furthered the need of new, radical approaches and gave way to new pedagogies that foreground the production of space (Froud and Harris 2015). The drive to rethink design pedagogy by introducing more practice components and by adapting the curriculum to the new challenges of professional practice has triggered numerous curriculum changes in the past few years in the UK context. Educators acknowledged that the old-fashioned idea of the architect as a well-rounded jack-of-all-trades is to be reconsidered (Pringle and Porter 2015). Today, the pressing challenges of the new climatic regime, of wars and economic uncertainty prompt us to rethink anew the ontological and epistemic basis of design education and to actively remodel design pedagogy.

As an applied and skills-oriented discipline, architecture's traditional orientation has always been that of a professional education. No matter where architecture is taught – at traditional universities, technical universities or universities of applied sciences – design studio remains at the centre of knowledge production and active knowledge exchange. It has a central role for shaping the fundamental characteristics of the discipline and its pedagogy. Design practice has evolved from apprenticeship through to the Beaux-arts and then the Bauhaus traditions (Crinson and Lubbock 1994), and this has resulted in different types of studio teaching (Salama 1995, Green and Bonollo 2003).

The pedagogy of design studio and juries has been studied extensively from different perspectives (Anthony 1991, Dutton 1987, Schön 1984, 1985, Stevens 1995, Webster 2005). The most exemplary study of studio-situated reflexivity of professional schools draws on a pragmatist mode of enquiry (Dewey 1933) and argues that reflection-in-action, stands against the systematic, scientific, linear way of knowing (Schön 1983). Schön's theory of 'reflective practice' made a revolution in design anthropology founding a new epistemology of practice, by taking as its point of departure the competence and artistry already embedded in skilful practice (Schön 1987). Yet, Schön explicitly positioned the student's prior knowledge as 'invalid' for the task at hand and thereby perpetuated an abuse of power that is unhelpful to the development of architecture as a profession (Willenbrock 1991). Following on these lines of criticism, Webster (2007, 2008) and Mewburn (2009) claimed that Schön promoted an inadequate idea of design learning as a mostly passive process of observation and replication in which the teacher's main role is too 'correct' the student's work, rather than help them to develop or hone their skills. This implied a narrow notion of how learning takes place through formal interactions only and failed to recognise the other dimensions of learning in addition to the cognitive – the affective and corporeal learning experiences and the student's potential to be an active learner. The idea of the studio as solely occupied by students and teachers was also questioned.

The current trend towards practice-orientation makes us rethink some of the key foundations of studio teaching, the distinctive knowledge cultures involved in it and the strategies for better adaptation of designers' education to the social and economic challenges of the day. Challenging further and adding to Schön's anthropology of design education, here we aim at analysing the 'performative' dimension of studio pedagogy and at generating an alternative account of its distinctive 'epistemic culture' (Knorr-Cetina 1999). Drawing on Actor-Network-Theory (ANT) inspired observation of the practice of the AA Interprofessional Studio (AAIS) – a post-professional programme leading to either a MA or MFA in Spatial Performance and Design – directed by Theo Lorenz and Tanja Siems, we will analyse it as an exemplar to critically evaluate the current forms of architectural pedagogy in the UK context. Recent studies of architectural practices took inspiration from ANT and paid close attention to the material, epistemic and social dimensions of design practice (Houdart and Minato 2009, Loukissas 2012, Latour and Yaneva 2008, Yaneva 2009a and 2009b) and yet, design pedagogy has been rarely explored from this perspective.

> We ask: 'What is the specific role of design studio at the intersection of research innovation and multiple social, economic and cultural networks embedded in design?' This will imply gaining better understanding of how the AAIS conducts design research and mobilises a large network of interlocutors from different disciplines. We will also reflect on the content and the skills taught at studio level, the partnerships, the spatial and material arrangements of the programmes, and the impact of various interprofessional networks on its design pedagogy. We will argue that the AAIS crafts a distinct epistemic culture whilst connecting a wide range of professionals and their social and economic networks in the relational orbits of a distinctive interprofessional knowledge production.

The Spaces that Make us Think

We will outline first the wider institutional context, relationships with other disciplines and spatial organisation of the AAIS. The spatial qualities and material arrangements of the programme (where it takes place – its studios and lecture rooms – and how it is affected by these spaces) affect the way students learn and interact. Moussavi's analytic comparison of the Architectural Association (AA) and the Harvard Graduate School of Design (GSD) is very revealing in this regard (2012). The spatial arrangement and pedagogical strategy of design schools, she argues, influence the kind of character students take on in the future. In what follows we will analyse how the spatial topographies of teaching and learning in the AAIS help shaping distinctive design cultures and students' profiles.

3.1
Seminar Session of Tanja Siems and Vera San
Payo de Lemos during the Spatial Narrative
Workshop in the AAIS studio 2022. (TL)

3.2
Oliver Van De Hen discussing with
students during the Staging and
Acting Workshop in 2022. (TL)

3.3
/people seminar with Theo Lorenz
and Tanja Siems in the studio with
students 2022. (TS)

3.4
Final discussion of the after the performance
of the results of the "Spatial Narrative"
Workshop with the audience. (TS)

3.5
Students developing performance for the
performance presentation of the Spatial
Narrative workshop in the studio. (TS)

The AAIS studio has always worked as a project office linked to a network of spaces and venues, and with this to various institutions and partners. The setting of the studio itself, however, has evolved over time. At the outset of the programme, as a course of ten students, the studio space was separated from the event spaces. The studio space served as a basic hub of design and collaboration, however for the applied parts of the studio additional spaces within the school were booked and transformed into short-term event spaces. In its current form of over thirty students the AAIS works from within a venue hub where smaller events and rehearsals can take place themselves. The applied nature of the studio differentiates the work from any usual pedagogic setting and the modus operandi is constantly changing between teaching and applying the work. Through the interdisciplinary work the studio model can neither follow a model of performance art, where the focus is on the rehearsal of performative work, nor that of a design studio with a setting focused on design around a table nor that of an artist studio, where the work would focus on the production of artefacts. The AAIS studio is a hybrid and constantly changing model between all these existing models. In this way the studio's space is transforming from practice rooms and rehearsal spaces to design studio, production workshop, teaching space and public events. This transformative action within one or multiple spaces becomes one of the core exercises and skills developed by the students and its team, a constant change between fixed settings and flux.

How is the AAIS organised and how it works?

As a post-professional programme, the AAIS explores alternative forms of collaboration between the multiple creative professions through the research, conception, design and implementation/production of a series of genre-defying spatial performances and constructions. By creating unique project-events that form the basis for continued discussion, the AAIS provides students with a starting point for individual careers within a new overarching discipline.

The programme provides through seminars, studio work, workshops and applied events a postgraduate programme that is based on interprofessional collaboration across the creative disciplines. The work of the studio demonstrates a field of work that stretches beyond the established professions and in this way creates projects within an 'in-between' discipline that is more than just the mere addition to the existing. To apply this work ethos, every year AAIS designs, curates and constructs events across the creative fields, such as dance, theatre and music performances, exhibitions, or festivals.

The programme is structured into two phases. The first phase concentrates on design studios and seminar-based teaching of the history and theory of interdisciplinary and interprofessional collaboration as well as network-based design, organisation and the realisation of applied events and installations resulting from the various collaborations. The second phase concentrates on the individual thesis of the students either in written form for the Master of Art students or through applied practice the in case of the Master of Fine Arts Students.

As an area of investigation, the field of performance offers itself as an ideal testing ground and laboratory for a wide field of design and architecture, as it bundles many of the main tasks within larger and smaller design projects and it clearly depended on a large level of layered collaborations. In a performance-based project the production must be delivered on time, to budget, with the given resources, managing a wide network of actants.

The approach of the studio can be seen as a fast-forward imitation of the experience process, we go through in practice, a boot-camp for networking and creation. As such the studio seeks to start for each individual a process where the given frameworks of the studio gradually transform into multiplying networks for each participant.

Initiatives and networks can easily overlap with different sets of aims and tasks whilst creating synergies within the overlap and divergences beyond. A simple example can be found within the different phases of the students in the studio and the studio itself. Whereas phase one focuses to discover the methodologies of the studio and to realise the first project, the second phase concentrates on building new networks, and a basis for one's own career. The alumni, in parallel, starts to realise independent projects, applying the newly learned skills in the much harder environment of practice. Meanwhile, the studio itself and its protagonists develop the academic and professional agenda on the basis of all three phases. None of these entities can exist in isolation from the other, needing the synergy between them to thrive, yet each has its own set of aims and stipulations.

This process unfolds within the duration of the course in three phases. In a first skilling phase a series of discipline or area of investigation related workshops take place, each manifesting in a public performance presentation. The collaboration takes place in a phase where the individuals in the teams still would have to discover their abilities and those of their peers. Yet, in the short time span of two weeks students develop and realise full projects based on the guidance and experience of the respective tutors. In rapid succession students learn in different settings how to organise themselves, how to negotiate ideas in relation to often new tasks and how to deliver these projects in a professional manner.

In a second phase students develop two successive larger performance festivals in collaboration with their tutors. The acquired skills now need to be applied within an overall given brief and with the local and international network and partners of the studio. These projects require multiple levels of collaboration in design, organisation and execution. In a final educational step, each student forms in a third phase on the basis of the previous experiences their individual future mode of working and networks.

In the case of the Master of Arts, degree students use the previous events as applied case stories to further explore theoretical possibilities of working within networked creative disciplines. The Master of Fine Arts degree students move on to create their first, individually applied project in practice. For this they have to ensemble their own collaboration networks, develop the full spectrum of the envisioned work including their project brief, budget, venue, and dissemination of the project. In both cases it is the main aim that the thesis project creates a lasting effect for the individual's professional future and initiates their networks through proven evidence.

In this way we facilitate an independent open outcome in frameworks of education for the students and alumni and form the basis of their individual responsibility. Moreover, teaching at the AAIS happens in an international network. These frameworks need to enable students to gain knowledge through applied projects with tangible lasting effects and allow them to build their individual networks for successful experiences moving forward.

Inter-professionalism in Action

Today's studio is based on transdisciplinarity (Doucet and Janssens 2010) and requires a much more complex setting of group learning environment that involves a larger number of actors. Drawing on transdisciplinarity, the AAIS programme offers a 'performative' take on pedagogical practices (Mewburn 2012) that assumes that the process of learning to 'think like an architect/designer/performing artist' implies a *composite network* where the design teacher(s) is one of many participants in design pedagogy. Design teaching and learning involves different actors – people, policies, tools, representations, learning environments, material arrangements, and spatial devices. The studio has a complex spatial setting where different temporalities and spatial arrangements coalesce; it offers a dual context of learning about design and learning to design, one that endorses and cultivates through teaching a specific attention to the performativity of design.

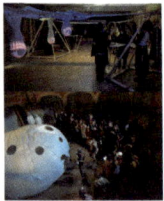

Designers today are also 'browsing practitioners' (Yaneva 2010, 2012) that surf large amounts of data; the studio is heavily influenced by computational methods (McCullough, Mitchell and Purcell 1990). In addition, students work *in messy material environments* that no longer involve sketches and drawings only, but a larger amount of hybrid objects (simulations, tests, video and sound recordings, material samples, experimental models, precedents, archival documents). Instead of being a site of asymmetric reflective practice, or power-based coaching, studio teaching, as we will illustrate here with the case of the AAIS, happens as an actor-network that often extends the existing networks of the school (of the AA) and the city that hosts it (London). Therefore, it cannot be studied in isolation as the studio pedagogy responds to it, but also crafts multifarious social and political connections. The studio thus has an important role in translating and generating research at the intersection between curriculum innovations and the wider AA networks in relation both with the city social and economic realities and the profession. Let us examine closely how the AAIS functions.

No Genius, but Collectives

When it comes to the creative disciplines the individual is all too often the focus of attention as the creator behind a project. However, this singling out of an individual from within a wider network of actants distracts us from the actual dynamics of the creative process. Instead, we should see what enables collaborations and what sets them in motion. What qualities and responsibilities are being cultivated with collaboration? How do we reach a creative result that benefits from the contributions of all participants in the network? How do collaborative networks form and transform over time? Here we need to ask further what basic ethics and responsibilities everyone should adhere to be able to create in a collaborative way?

It is not easy to translate initial ideas into an actual project. The process might seem to be even more difficult if one must rely on a network of collaborators. Yet, following the activities of the AAIS we witness that the collaborative network helps the idea to evolve, to mature and to gain richer qualities. Moreover, there is no fixed idea at the start and realised as such at the end. In reality, ideas evolve through many detours and variations from the initial scenario due to numerous factors that impinge on the project and the multiple new partnerships that are being shaped in the process. Even the greatest works of art, we know it after Alpers (1982), like the paintings of Rembrandt were not marked by the loneliness of human conditions but rather by the hectic activity in his studio. The ways the work of the studio is organised, the atmosphere and the social life in the studio (the critics, the collaborators, and hired artists, the providers, etc.) all have an impact on the creative work, on the collaborative process and on the final content of the works. At the AAIS one never creates in isolation, in solitude, but always surrounded by people, and supported by a hybrid network of practitioners.

In this network made of artists, performers, architects, designers, musicians, and dancers the difference is celebrated. Everyone brings its own talent, niche expertise and ambitions to the group and invests these into the overall outcome. Like in a music ensemble it is however necessary to have an intrinsic understanding of the overall. If everyone in an ensemble would be a 'first violin' we would have a result that would be merely an overloaded rendition of a part of an overall composition, where each violin tries to sound out the others. If each musician has their own individual instruments, the entire piece can be played. Yet if the lead violin still would want to show that it is superior to the other musicians the result would be very uneven and unpleasant. Only if the entire ensemble is aware of the strengths and weaknesses of all its members can a harmonious performance be achieved. Each talent is given the space to unfold their art, yet they know when to give space to the other talents. This ability to give space to others and to share, is according to Hannah Arendt (Arendt 1958), what makes a society function.

In the collective format of work, it is impossible for everyone to work on the same aspect of the project. Collaborative networks provide opportunities to work on specific tasks at hand whilst offering an opportunity to grasp and understand the overall ambition of the project at the same time; an ability to simultaneous focus and see the entirety at a glance. Whereas the ideas can shift frequently within the process, through 'circulating references' (Latour 1999, 27-74) the overall framework expands and transforms over time.

3.6
Performance Presentation of the Choreography
Workshop led by New Movement Collective
2019 in the AA Barrel Vault. (TL)

3.7
Audience participation during
the "2121.2.1.0" Performance at
"Camden Market" 2020. (TL)

3.8
Inflatable structure during the
"Portrait of Humans" performance
at the "Nest" in London. (TS)

3.9
Video installation as part of the
performance presentation of the
Dramaturgy Workshop 2022. (TL)

3.10
Final performance presentation of
the "Spatial Narrative" Workshop
2022 in the AAIS studio. (TL)

3.11
David McAlmont in final discussion
with students before the performance
presentation of the "Sound" workshop. (TL)

The ideal outcome of a collective work allows for a recognisable overall product in all its components and contributions, whilst, at the same time, allowing us to zoom into partial intersections or individual areas, with the same professional benchmarks we would apply to them in isolation. The purpose of collaboration is to discover overlaps and opportunities. Whereas all AAIS projects follow this principle a good example of this process can be seen in the project of "Portrait of Human" (AAIS, 2018) at the Stone Nest in Soho. Through a series of hybrid characters that reflected various aspects of human behaviour and vanity as TV-human, mirror-human and plastic-human the performance aimed to reveal the essence of what it is to be human in a constantly changing world. Whereas all participants of the team were artist, designers or architects each member had multiple yet specific areas of expertise and interests. One student focused on structural design and setup, another concentrated on the structure and stage with the development of costume in mind, a third one collaborated on the costumes by extending the work into video and interactive projections. A fourth student worked on connecting the visual material to light design and music scores, whereas the fifth student took the responsibility for choreography and sequence in collaboration with the sixth student who worked on the design, the organisation as well as the concept and the narrative. None of these areas of activities were privileged. Instead, all of them tangled together and formed an intense cycle of exchange throughout the activities and their extensive documentation. The synergies between all these activities formed an overall network of design components that formed an intriguing and innovative project.

In this way, multiple initiatives can unfold synchronously, and synergies can be created. The results therefore will no longer represent just one homogeneous body of work, one niche expertise, but rather an unfolding heterogeneous network of creative practice. Each component can be appreciated on its own, however its full potential unfolds within the overlap dynamic of the composite work of art. In such a setting the work stays fluid. Individual components and subsets can develop over time, at different speed, emerge, disappear, or even branch off to become independent or a subset for other ensembles. Through the dynamic collaborations the collective of students with different artistic know-how gains the freedom to develop the project into multiple directions, to define different specific subsets, and to test new emerging opportunities.

Learning Based on Evidence and Shared Experience

The collaborative approach is more difficult to teach, as it depends on experience and the ability to connect meaningfully in an educational setting. It is not enough to follow an approach of merely teaching hypothetical content, but rather always prove collaboratively with the students the theoretical assumptions through evidence and shared experience. Within the context of performance this evidence is delivered through the applied projects. Spatial performances in front of a 'witnessing' audience must be realised and delivered on time with all its wanted, and 'un-wanted' components in place at the moment. Whilst embedded in a continuous process before and after the 'show' the performance itself is what is in front of you. The result is tangible and immediate and can be accessed by all participants of the process. Audience and creators can evaluate the project based on what they have experienced together, allowing for critique and debate to take place for the next iterations of projects to come.

This approach of course is not new. John Dewy proposed in the first half of the last century an education that is based on actual experience, where knowledge is no longer taught as predetermined norms and historical information, handed down by the educator, but rather based on actual, shared, and continued experience between tutors and students (Dewey 1938). This way of education became applied in various educational environments, most notably the "Black Mountain College", founded among others by John Andrew Rice. Here creative practitioners from various disciplines and standings like Josef Albers, Buckminster Fuller, Merce Cunningham and John Cage used tangible projects to create these actual experiences with their peers and students. Dewey noted that the social and physical conditions of education are crucial and therefore become a main task for the educators to provide.

Within the AAIS all projects are based on an applied approach set within a wider network of creative practitioners, institutions, and disciplines. The scope of the creative process varies considerably from product design to large-scale architecture. Often the projects cannot be fully realised in educational environment, but their key important aspects are tested, proved and developed, and this can have a lasting effect on the career of the students from various cultural and disciplinary backgrounds.

Building Skills for Expanding Networks

Preparing the students for work across different disciplines within creative networks requires us to teach them how to find initiatives and to build one's own network. These skills are developed step by step, starting from a guided, taught environment and leading towards the creation of an individual professional career path. The educational process here is built up in three main steps of applied projects: first 'skilling', second 'guided' collaborations for the production of specific events and finally, 'project-delivery' that also leads to the crafting of a specific network.

3.12
Katie Burks wearing the costume for the "TV-human" as part of the "Portrait of Humans" performance at the "nest" London. (TS)

3.13
Effie Gu is fitting the costume for the "TV human" character Katie Burks of "Portrait of Humans" 2019. (TS)

3.14
Performance of Mirror Human and Bubble Human inside the inflatable structure. (TS)

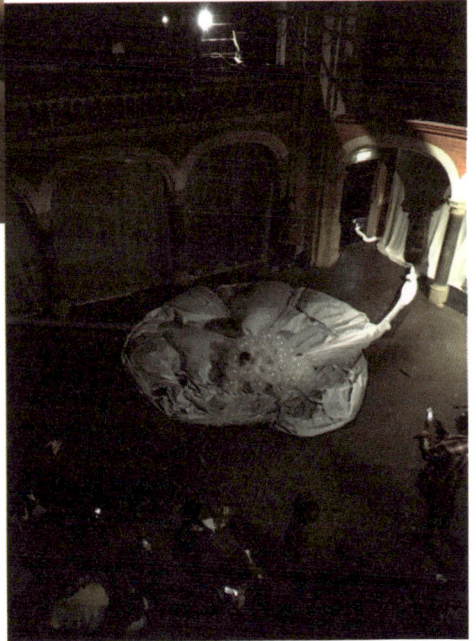

3.15
View through the window
towards the performance inside
the inflatable structure. (TL)

3.16
Performance on the deflated
structure in the centre of
the "Nest". (TS)

In the first phase of 'skilling' students are taught in a series of workshops to deliver within two to three weeks projects related to specific disciplines and practice such as Film and Narrative, Sound and Music, Stage and Performance and Choreography by professionals from the respective discipline. Students get to know how to work within the set of criteria of each of the different genres. As most of them have no previous experience with these specific topics, they start working outside their usual comfort zone and rely on the knowledge of the tutors and peers. Yet, they bring their own set of experiences to the task. During this initial phase students are thrown into new networks and areas of investigation. They must rapidly learn not only to pick up new skills, but also how to communicate these new skills with professionals and others around them. During this process, however, students rely on the previous knowledge and skills they have brought to the studio and apply them to a specific given topic. In such an environment, for instance, a modelling tool might be applied to a sound workshop, or a type of fashion design might become the forming factor for a choreography workshop. This process challenges the existing best practice of each discipline from the outset. As a result, the final performances of these workshops depend not only on the given genre, but even more on the set of individuals with their specific skills thrown together in a new adventure.

In the second phase, the learning process is no longer based on skilling rooted in discrete disciplinary knowledge but is instead focused on producing specific events within the outlined brief of the studio (Lorenz 2016). The events happen within larger networks, thus extending the group of peers and tutors from various disciplines to a wider network of local and international partner institutions and venues. The events are by default experimental, often unprecedented due to the unexpected mixture of disciplines enrolled. Each year these events are the key engine driving creativity and innovation within the programme. Each event builds upon and extends the experiences acquired in the previous year. Students work as a team on all parts of the implementation of the year's events. They work on the hands-on fabrication of the sets and exhibition artefacts in close collaboration with experts of the relevant field. They also carry out the installation of required technologies and direct the organisation and management of the performances.

The first event in the series takes place with a limited scope, budget, and time and thus the ideas and experimentation of the studio are subject to intense reality testing. For this the studio works with collaborative partners throughout Europe. The team can study the elements that worked or did not work and develop the design ideas and their methods on an actual applied project, rather than a hypothetical approach. The team can draw clear conclusions from the experience and know-how to be able to reapply them within a different environment.

The second event, conducted typically in collaboration with a renowned international partner, builds up on the components of the previous event. Here the unique results of the first event can be extended, varied, and transformed without losing its experimental character. This happens on all levels of the year's design project. The structures get extended to become main spatial environments, the music, dramaturgy, and choreography gets more elaborated and rehearsed and the method of documenting the process allows for more precision and creative variation. The overall project is placed within a specific socio-political environment as a testing ground.

Crucially the events series contribute to the crafting of networks and context, and ultimately open up possibilities for the students to develop their individual areas of investigation and skills. They also begin to make connections enabling them to build a wider network of allies for their projects. For this reason, the students are encouraged to test and discuss the events with the local community and different audiences through workshops and other related activities.

The final and third phase is the 'project-delivery' that also leads to the crafting of a specific network. This forms at the same time the initial phase of a professional career. This could develop either as a theoretical exploration and research (for the Master of Arts students), based on the actual case studies and experience of the first phases, or as an applied project (for the Master of Fine Arts students). Fundamentally, both directions of work need to be based on actual evidence and applied knowledge. On this basis both final outputs depend on multifarious networks of input and collaboration, and a concluding evidential after-effect. Moreover, they should also create new initiatives and demonstrate a way forward for the students and their newly established network.

3.17/18/19/20
Students testing objects and artefacts during the collaborative workshop and with
the MA/MFA choreography programme of Trinity Laban in 2018 and 2019. (TL)

3.21
Mock-TV show "Profiling History" as result of the Narrative
workshop 2018 at the Architectural Association. (TL)"

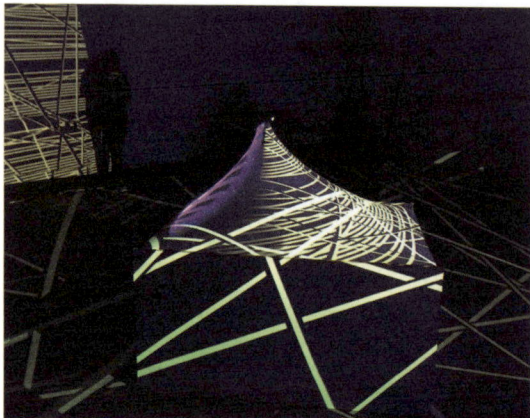

3.22
Projection on performing-fabric during the
"choreography" workshop of New Movement
Collective as part of the "UnReal" brief 2015. (TS)

3.23
Projection field during the performance
presentation of the Dramaturgy and film
workshop 2019 at the AA Barrel Vault. (TL)

3.24
"Others" presentation as results
of the sound workshop with
Andy Dean 2018. (TL)

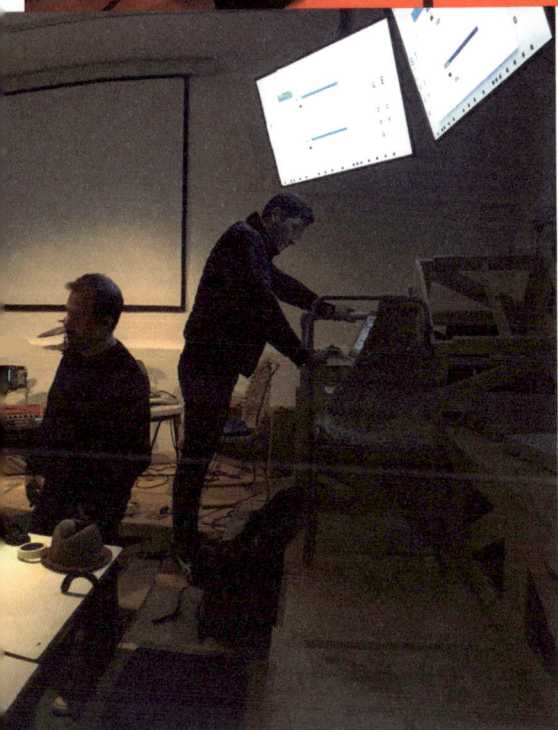

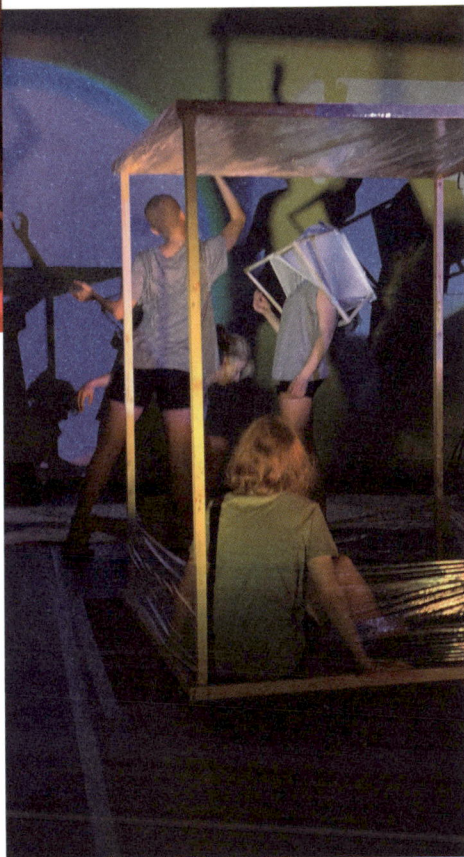

3.25
Andy Dean discussing with the musicians
and students a series of sound experiments
during the sound workshop in 2014. (TL)

3.26
Performance presentation "TORQUE" in the AAIS studio as
the result of the choreography workshop by New Movement
Collective with Patrcia Okenwa and Joe Walkling 2022. (TS)

In this phase students no longer can rely on 'holding hands' with the studio, but rather need to independently build their own conceptual frameworks and practical networks to support their thesis projects using the skills and experience of the previous events. For the applied projects, for instance, the students have to form their own team to deliver the project. They have to craft a detailed plan that covers all steps – from the project brief to budget. Moreover, they have to think about all aspects – the venue, the design, the materiality, among others. They must assemble performers, co-creators and supporters to deliver a full public project to a professional standard. In the process of doing this, they become designers, entrepreneurs, producers and often as well performers at the same time, thus setting up the foundation of a professional career. The results are unique in their scope and individual after-effect.

In what follows, we refer to a range of exemplar projects developed by AAIS alumni who now teach on the course and continue to contribute to and expand the studio's approach across both academia and practice. We focus in particular on their use of networks and the formation practices they have developed in relation to their individual projects.

Space as a Narrative

The MA thesis "The Story of Space: A Narrative and its Disorder" (Shemer 2018) of the architect and journalist Hila Shemer was independently a story and at the same time a construction of space. The narrative achieved to write space. Hila emphasises the importance of architectural writing being intimately connected to physical structures and the material world. She employs both the tools of an architect and a writer in her research, aiming to explore the relationship between space and storytelling in various disciplines. As 'building material' Hila used the evidence of the various case studies of the work she has been part of during the first phases of the studio, as the 'mortar' she used case studies that extended the argument and as the 'blueprints' the different pathways and networks of her personal life. Together she created an intrinsic network of thoughts that expanded in all dimensions, allowing the reader to move through it at one's own pace, direction, and time. The written work did not need an introduction, abstract or conclusion as it created through evidence a multitude of possible after-effects in relation to the reader and their own networks. Hila developed her work of spatial narratives both as a journalist with over four hundred published articles as well as an educator both at the Bezalel Academy in Jerusalem as well as at the AA School in London.

Bridging the Divide Between the Performing Subjects and Stage Objects

The stage designer and architect Mona Camille designed her written thesis "What is the necessary degree of design" as an applied laboratory to research the effectiveness of minimal design within the setting of stage design (Camille 2018). On the basis of her experience gained through the previous events, she created a series of small interventions as testing grounds of audience reactions to different spatial arrangements between set and performer. She researched the relation between the performing subjects and the surrounding objects and how these enabled lasting impact on the extended networks of audience, site, and surroundings. The results and established evidence created for her the basis of further work, both in practice as a stage designer collaborating closely with artist and performers, but also in academia where she created together with Oliver van de Hen the workshop module of 'staging artist', an intrinsic part of the skilling phase of the studio and the development of cross-disciplinary communication.

Expanding the Networks

The artist Argyris Angeli and producer Kyriaki Nasioula continued their successful collaboration of the first phase of the studio founding as the framework for their final project "Ithaca" the performance company "GesamtAtelier" (Angeli, Nasioula 2017). "Ithaca" is an inter-media performance/installation that explores the impact of increasing cultural flows on individuals, examining how they voluntarily or involuntarily move across geographical areas for various reasons and navigate between different creative fields, aiming to integrate into new destinations and redefine their identity, relationship with space, time, and others. They started the process to set up as a performance company by developing the group project of their phase 1 as XYZ/s extended and winning the UK Young Artists National Festival. Based on these networks, they developed their project "Ithaca" linking their work back to further networks of collaborators in their home countries of Greece and Cyprus. The many iterations of the performance became a powerful initiator for continuously growing networks of collaborators and partners, leading to new projects, partnerships, and productions. Each successful development served as evidence for new support and exposure of their work as evident in GesamtAtelier's latest project "loom". Together Argyris and Kyriaki teach production based on network creation and concept development, bridging artistic approach and applied delivery of projects.

3.27
Students working on installation of extendable
arch at Hooke park in Dorsett for "Trust, Truth,
Integrity" performance. (TS)

3.28/29/30
"Trust, Truth, Integrity" performances with sand stage,
plant based buffet and interactive tripods at the
"Testbed Two" in Bermondsey London in 2014. (TS)

3.31
New Movement Collective performing
AAIS's "The Conversation" in 2013 at the
"Barge House" at London's Southbank. (TS)

3.32
Hila Shemers setting up her wall of questions in the
front members room of the Architectural Association
as part of her MA final Thesis in 2018. (TS)

3.33/34
Mona Camille's spatial setup for a street performance
with Olivier van Den Hende as part of her applied test
for her MA Thesis project in 2018. (TL)

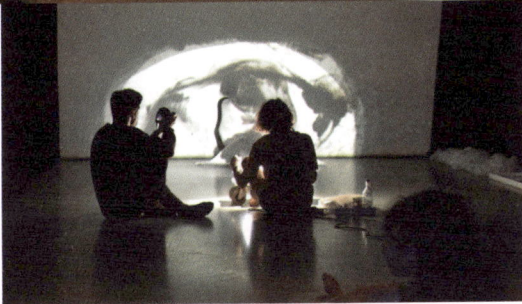

3.35/36/37
"Ithaca" MFA thesis project performances by Kyriaki
Nasioula and Argyris Angeli at the Roehampton Theatre
and the Architectural Association in London 2017. (TL)

3.38
Sound installation with Yoshiki Ichihara
as part of "Schweigen & Sprechen"
MFA thesis project by Noa Segev. (TL)

3.39
"Schweigen & Sprechen" MFA thesis
performance with Nina Traub at the
Camden Market by Noa Segev in 2019. (TL)

Networks of the Past/ Networks of the Future

As a final case study of network development, we will discuss the work of Noa Segev. The thesis "Schweigen & Sprechen" (Segev 2018) of Noa was based on her own family's history. Every component of the project was used as active material within the project. The story of her great-grandfather creating the renowned glass company "Weisswasser" in Germany enabled a collaboration with the current company of Still glass and provided the base of 'fragile' material for the story of the Jewish family giving up its home and fleeing the persecution in Germany to Israel. The conflict of the family expressed itself in a careful choreographed performance and installation that held all components at a constant balance and in an open, fragile, yet alarming dialogue.

The sensibility of dealing with the many factors of a personal story extended to a sensibility of careful collaboration within multiple networks: the family, the collaborators, and the extended audience. Action and communication became parts of the same continuum. This skill of careful, yet active negotiation and communication is the basis of Noa's expertise today as a creator and educator both at the Bezalel Academy and within the AAIS.

What the different projects of the alumni of the course have in common is to actively build forward-looking networks of collaborations across the work that constantly feed back to the networks of the studio. Therefore, the studio's network itself is constantly extending, bifurcating and growing, actively influencing the approach of the AAIS for each new generation.

Bringing People Together through Design

Cultural and creative projects have proven to be viable tools to create consent and advocacy through active participation of otherwise estranged or opposing parties (Siems, Lorenz 2023, Chapter 01).

The possibilities of creating events that provide an area of overlap within a wide spectrum of interest and perceptions enables creatives to bring people and groups together that otherwise might not be able or would resist to share experiences. These potentially take the responsibility of design far beyond the responsibility toward the collaborative and active network but extends it further into society at large.

The activities of AAIS also have a huge impact and provide opportunities to develop. The AAIS philosophy demonstrates that interdisciplinary projects have transformative abilities on a cultural level that go beyond the narrow framework of the direct stakeholders of the projects, and they often become the springboard of new creative initiatives. Design projects have a relational power – they bring people together, initiate new collaborations and developments beyond their initial brief and trigger long-lasting effects. The AAIS initiatives range between culinary experiences and pop-up markets to choreographical events across different countries. What they all have in common is that they have a tangible impact that can be traced backward and forward in relation to the interaction of the studio and students.

To best illustrate this process, we can refer to the project "The Angle of Incidence" at the Matadero Madrid in 2011 (AAIS 2011). This third intervention of the studio at the Matadero Madrid focused on how the local community of the former slaughterhouse area could reconnect to the site and start to form a productive symbiosis with the new cultural centre and its audience. The project was from the outset set up to create multiple points of interaction staging not only a performance, but also multiple layers of collaborative workshops and activities in areas of shared interest between the different constituencies.

Each element actively linked local components with a wider set of networks. The performance integrated not only professional performers from London, Cologne and Madrid, but also invited participants of an organised dance workshop to be part of the overall performance itself. The performance was embedded in a network of workshops and activities centred on the culinary history of the site. A dinner was organised for local and international artists to meet, discuss and to engage in new dialogues. The food was prepared by local restaurants in collaboration with the studio. This culinary network was extended by a market that was staged within the setting of the performance where local producers could offer their goods. Still today the involved restaurants remain present on the site and the market takes place on a regular basis. The crafted relations remain durable.

Tools and Techniques

Within an interprofessional network of talents and disciplines a new set of knowledge emerges with each new collaboration and project. This entails new ways of working and procurement, but also tools and materials that form an intrinsic part of the overall execution of the AAIS projects. In such an environment no set of tools or rules is fixed as they would be in a single discipline. The best practice of one discipline will always be challenged and tested through the other disciplines involved and as such its tools will be re-appropriated and adjusted to find areas of deployment. AAIS does not engage in teaching specific tools or sets of software to students, but rather guide students on how to learn, approach, use or combine software and tools as required by the specificity of their projects. Here the scheduling tasks of performances and logistics go hand in hand with 3D, virtual reality and interactive design software, choreography, and music scores as well as video and light design, each category challenging the veracity of the other. The resulting artefacts of design, their production and installation are the manifestation of the interplay of all these elements.

Whereas each individual project and its underlying process can be described as an interplay between a range of networked tools, the XYZ (AAIS 2017) project stands out as an example. The project implies a series of events that consisted of a combination of choreography, live video mapping and projections as well as a set of reconfigurable stage components. Each of the elements depended on a careful exchange with each of the other components resulting in a highly precise sequence of events. The core of the production was the live interplay of performers, audience and stage objects through live video loops and connections. The markers on stage were formed as a set of three-dimensional nodal points of a flexible and reconfigurable grid. These were designed as 2D patterns that could be assembled into a 3D node. As the production took place across four different venues across Europe, the 2D patterns could be sent ahead for CNC milling on location allowing for the construct to grow throughout the process. Scheduling and 'cues' became the main task during the performance; equally, moments of exchange during the production ensured synchronicity in the procurement of each component of the event.

Ecological Concerns

The power of creative work to form a common ground and to actively create togetherness beyond our direct networks gains an even greater urgency in the new climatic regime. This makes us rethink pedagogy as a tool to entice a behavioural change away from 'use' and 'extraction' of resources, and towards creativity, togetherness and compassion.

The AAIS facilitates a compassionate collaborative togetherness to unfold to allow individuals to thrive and re-gain balance with our environment. Whereas cultural projects often might address urgent issues and achieve lasting after-effects, their realisation often does not fully address sustainable concerns within their production and execution itself to an equal level. Material procurement, production means, reuse, continued use, energy sufficiency and transport, but also team organisation accommodation and sustainable catering for the team, all needs to be part of a continued discourse of sustainable culture (Buro Happold 2022). The project series of "Three Graces" at the Theatre Abierto in Lisbon addressed this topic in detail, testing, and evaluating each component of the process for its overall environment. Small details make a considerable difference, such as a consequent use of exclusively scrap material as in the "Seed to Scene" where all material was sourced form offcuts of timber mills and CNCed leftover plywood. Equally, in the case of the inflatable structures in the "Exquisite Corpse" project small leftovers of fabric were used from the production line of the company "Inflate". Additionally, resources can be bundled by combining transport in hand luggage, catering and food can be procured locally, plant-based material can be used for all projects of the studio abroad. This environmental awareness is at the heart of all AAIS projects.

Conclusions

Following the work of the AAIS we can argue there is no clear division between 'design/art/dance/music/performance' on the one hand, and 'society/economy/culture' aspects, on the other. Instead, they are closely entangled. Art/design is not the special creation of an individual genius, but the mundane product of a dense and versatile networks of co-operations (Baxandall 1972, Becker 1982) between different participants: partners, advisers, materials, external contractors, markets, local suppliers, international organisations, etc. Moreover, the dynamic environment of the AAIS showcases that there are many 'intermediaries' between the work of art/design/performance and the broader context/ society: collaborators, alumni, artistic techniques and technologies, critics, materials, organisations, precedents, local communities, and institutions. Scrutinising the participation of all actors, both human and non-human, involved in this process, and highlighting how they work together, their role and impact on the creative process, we have shed light on the distinctive network-inspired pedagogical philosophy of the AAIS. Instead of being product-driven, the studio succeeds in cultivating distinctive skills of crafting active networks and collaborations through applied projects. The careful negotiation and advocacy become unique identifiable elements of the style of all AAIS works. The collaborations emerging from the studio are open, innovative, inviting, and inclusive and at the same time assertive, active, efficient, and fearless. Its networks extend, bifurcate, combine, and interlink creating continuously new initiatives. They become, to paraphrase Michael Baxandall (1972) a deposit of social relationships and reflect and shape back the multiple social connections crafted in the studio.

3.40
"Superposition" as part of the "XYZ" series at the Architecture
Center of the MuseumsQuartier, in Vienna 2016. (VB)

3.41/42
XYZ performance at the Watermans Arts Centre,
London 2016. (VB)

References

Alpers, Svetlana (1982), Rembrandt's Enterprise: The Studio and the Market. University of Chicago Press.

Angeli, Argyris & Nasioula, Kyriaki, (2017) 'Ithaca' AAIS MFA Thesis Project, Architectural Association School of Architecture (AA), London

Anthony, Kathryn H. (1991) Design Juries on Trial: The Renaissance of the Design Studio. New York: Van Nostrand Reinhold.

Arendt, Hannah (1958) 'The Human Condition', University of Chicago Press.

Baxandall, Michael (1972) 'Painting and Experience in 15th century Italy', Oxford University Press.

Becker, Howard (1982) 'Art Worlds', University of California Press.

Buro Happold, (2022), 'The Theatre Green Book, Volume 1-3: Sustainable Productions, Buildings and Operations', [https://theatregreenbook.com] downloaded on 20.02.2023.

Camille, Mona (2018) 'What is the necessary degree of design' AAIS MA Thesis Project, Architectural Association School of Architecture (AA), London

Crinson and Lubbock (1994) 'Three Hundred Years of Architectural Education in Britain'. Manchester: Manchester University Press

Cuff, Dana (1991) 'Architecture: The Story of Practice'. Cambridge. MA: Massachusetts Institute of Technology.

Dewey, John (1938) 'Experience and Education', Collier Books, NY

Dewey, John (1933) 'How We Think: A Restatement of the Relation of Reflective Thinking to the Educative Process'. New York: Heath.

Doucet, Isabelle and Janssens, Nel (2010) 'Transdisciplinary Knowledge Production in Architecture and Urbanism. Towards hybrid modes of inquiry'. Vienna, New York: Springer.

Dutton, Thomas. A. (1987) 'Design and studio pedagogy', in Journal of Architectural Education 41(1): 16-25.

Froud and Harris (2015) 'Radical Pedagogies: Architectural Education and the British Tradition'. London: RIBA Publishing.

Green and Bonollo (2003) 'Studio-based teaching: history and advantages in the teaching of design', World Transactions on Engineering and Technology Education 2003 UICEE Vol.2, No.2, 2003, 269-272.

Knorr-Cetina, Karin (1999) 'Epistemic Cultures: How the Sciences Make Knowledge', Cambridge. Mass.: Harvard University Press.

Latour, Bruno (1999) 'Pandora's Hope' pp 24-79, Harvard University Press

Latour, Bruno and Woolgar S. (1979) Laboratory Life: The Social Construction of Scientific Facts. Beverly Hills: Sage Publications

Lorenz, Theo (2016) 'AAIS Coursebook', Architectural Association School of Architecture (AA), London

Loukissas, Yanni A. (2012) 'Co-Designers. Cultures of Computer Simulation in Architecture'. London and New York: Routledge.

McCullough, Mitchell and Purcell (1990) The Electronic Design Studio: Architectural Education in the Computer Era. Massachusetts: The MIT Press.

Mewburn, Inger (2009) 'Constructing bodies: gestures, speech and representation at work in architectural design studies'. Ph.D. thesis, University of Melbourne.

Mewburn, Inger (2012) 'Lost in translation: Reconsidering reflective practice and design studio pedagogy', in Arts and Humanities in Higher Education, n 11, pp 363.

Moussavi, Farshid 2012, 'School buildings produce culture', in 28th September Architectural Review [https://www.architectural-review.com/today/school-buildings-produce-culture] downloaded on 15.04.2023.

Nicol and Pilling (2000), 'Changing Architectural Education. Towards a new professionalism'. London and New York: E & FN Spon.

Pringle and Porter (2015), 'Education to reboot a failed profession', in Froud and Harris (ed.) Radical Pedagogies: Architectural Education and the British Tradition. London: RIBA Publishing.

Salama, Ashraf (1995) 'New Trends in Architectural Education: Designing the Design Studio'. Tailored Text & Unlimited Potential Publishing.

Schön, Donald A. (1983) 'The Reflective Practitioner: How Professionals Think in Action'. New York: Basic Books.

Schön, Donald A. (1984) 'The architectural studio as an exemplar of education for reflection-in-action', in Journal of Architectural Education 38(1): 2-9.

Schön, Donald A. (1985) 'The Design Studio: An Exploration of its Traditions and Potentials'. London: RIBA Publications.

Schön, Donald A. (1987) 'Educating the Reflective Practitioner'. San Francisco, CA: Jossey-Bass.

Segev, Noa (2019) 'Schweigen & Sprechen' AAIS MFA Thesis Project, Architectural Association School of Architecture (AA), London

Shemer, Hila (2018) 'The Story of Space', AAIS MA Thesis Project, Architectural Association School of Architecture (AA), London

Siems, Tanja (2023), 'Imparting City', Chapter 01 Common Ground with Theo Lorenz, Birkhäuser, Basel

Stevens, Garry (1995) 'Struggle in the studio: a Bourdivian look at architectural pedagogy', in Journal of Architectural Education 49(2): 105-22.

Webster, Helena (2005) 'A study of ritual, acculturation and reproduction in architectural education', in Arts and Humanities in Higher Education 4(3): 265-82.

Webster, Helena (2007) 'The analytics of power – Re-presenting the design jury', in Journal of Architectural Education 60(3): 21-7.

Webster, Helena (2008) 'Architectural education after Schön: Cracks, blurs, boundaries and beyond', in Journal for Education in the Built Environment 3(2): 63-74.

Willenbrock, Laura L. (1991) 'An undergraduate voice in architectural education, in T. A. Dutton (ed.) Voices in Architectural Education: Cultural Politics and Pedagogy. pp. 97-120, New York: Bergin & Garvey

Yaneva, Albena (2009a) 'The Making of a Building: A Pragmatist Approach to Architecture', Oxford: Peter Lang Publishers.

Yaneva, Albena (2009b) 'Made by OMA: An Ethnography of Design', Rotterdam: 010 Publishers.

Yaneva, Albena (2010) 'From Reflecting-in-Action Towards the Mapping of the Real', in Doucet, I. and Janssens, N. (eds.) Transdisciplinary Knowledge Production in Architecture and Urbanism. Towards hybrid modes of inquiry. Vienna, New York: Springer, pp. 117-128.

Project AAIS 2011-12, Event series 'Angles of Incidence' Elyse Agnelo, Lyndsey Housden, Jason Kofinas, Yelena Li, Architectural Association School of Architecture (AA), London

Project AAIS 2016-17, Event series 'XYZ's' Argyris Angeli, Kyriaki Nasioula, Justina Choli, Suh-in Park and Menglan Wu, Architectural Association School of Architecture (AA), London

Project AAIS 2018-19, Event series 'Portrait of Humans' Yuan Gu, Nasha Bahasoean, Lier Chen, Justine Mary De Penning, Denghui Lian, Aimee Rebecca Lam Tunon, Aijin Ying, Architectural Association School of Architecture (AA), London

Project AAIS 2014-15, Event series 'Moving Stone' Sumaya Islam, Dongsoo Koo, Mariana Vargas, Architectural Association School of Architecture (AA), London

Robin Hunt
Portia Kamons
Theo Lorenz
Tanja Siems

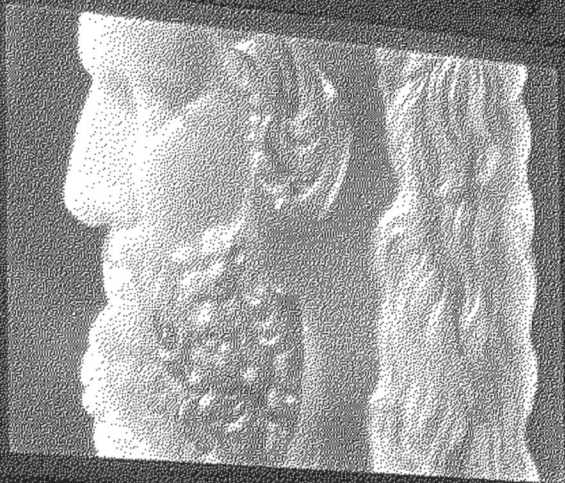

PERFORMANCE, PROTEST, POLITICS

The importance of Performance

Performance can take many forms and shapes; its actions can take place anywhere, on stage, on the street, on a screen, in a cave, at an office. Besides the performing arts such as theatre, dance, music, performance art, we can talk about performance at work, about how an object or structure is performing. We discuss this at length in the chapter "Object and performance". What all forms of performance share, however, is a delivery in relation to a given framework or set of tasks. It can thus for this chapter be argued that performance is the art of delivery. What we see and can try to measure, is how much is accomplished in relation to specific benchmarks or frameworks.

In Plato's allegory of the cave, the Greek philosopher describes a world in which **an imagined group of people forever chained facing inwards to the wall of a cave observe shadows projected from objects (or their own bodies) passing in front of light coming from behind them, the original movie-goers (Plato 2007 [380 BCE]). These people, together or separately, describe and name the shapes they see. These shadows are clearly not the real world: but in Plato's view they represent a, or the, framework of performed reality which we can normally perceive through our senses. These images are thus a performance – an art – which we interpret individually, collectively, or both.** The 'performance' of these shapes can be interpreted as 'the world' – or as a site-specific experience, it matters less than the process. The shadows deliver a story; the interpretation of the narrative of that story depends on the framework, and on the values of the people who consume the performance.

But how to evaluate any performance, from Plato's shadows to Nan Goldin's activism against the Sackler family in the major art galleries of the world? Because a performance is never neutral. It carries at all times consequences and responsibilities, values (relations to and with the performer, the location, the verbal and or visual language and vocabulary chosen and used). A performance that merely fulfils tasks, starts, continues, ends without questioning the value, veracity, and effect of its intentional, or unintentional, framework is likely to have less impact.

If the framework for observation is at odds with the creative intent of the performance with its authors and performers, even a good performance becomes an exercise in 'tick boxing' which results in no lasting transformative effect, or as David Graeber describes such a disjunction, it becomes a 'bullshit job' (Graeber 2018). We will return to the question of framework later in this chapter as many types can have destructive aims: a good performance which succeeds in delivering within this framework could accelerate a negative social effect, propaganda with a harmful agenda, for example. Consequently, a performance cannot be seen or critiqued in isolation.

Identical performances can immensely change in value, effect, and impact in relation to the frameworks by which they are judged, most obviously the framework of *time*. The post-Dada movement values inherent in Andre Breton's novel Nadja (Breton 1999 [1928]), and the myriad of performances based upon 'following people' around urban spaces, an idea that informs the early 1960s and 1970s work of the American performance artist Vito Acconci change radically in value, effect and impact considered today in the framework of #MeToo and 'surveillance culture'. Acconci's seminal situationist-influenced performances in the Streets of Manhattan or for small theatre audiences explored ideas of the body and public space. One of his most famous pieces was "The Following Piece" (Acconci 1969), in which for twenty-three days he selected random passers-by on New York City streets and followed them for as long as he was able – usually until they entered private property.

It is claimed, as it was for Breton, for Dada, that Acconci was opening the city into an operational space, a map. The Dadaist April 1921 group visit to Saint-Julien-le-Pauvre, its first 'action' in the Great Dada Season, took place before the idea of performance art existed, could be read as a parody of tourism, and the rudeness of its members as a rejection of bourgeois vulgarity (Richter and Britt 1978). Such performances as Acconci or Dada could now be considered not just transgressive but offensive, utterly impossible to produce, the artist as a 'stalker'. The social framework has changed.

For whilst it can be that the values and frameworks are in line with the creator's aim, enabling a performance that creates a more intense and more lasting effect, its language may not speak to its time; what was radical in 1969 might be impossible today; might be seen as threatening, requiring trigger warnings; perhaps even being 'illegal'. The case of the French artist Sophie Calle is perhaps more interesting as its legacy continues, and she still makes work. Influenced by Oulipo, the ideas of a 'constrained' art, a performance made within a quantifiably limited framework, Queneau once described Oulipians as 'rats who construct the labyrinth from which they plan to escape'. Calle takes the work of Acconci further into dramatically staged exhibitions, films and books. As her Tate biography states she: *"is recognised for her detective-like tendency to follow strangers and investigate their private lives"*(Tate Gallery 2024). She has developed the idea within narrative, documentary and photography to develop powerful performances. What does her action mean to audiences today? What questions does she raise, wandering the liminal spaces between art, biography, place, and photographic reproduction?

Interpretation, individually and collectively, can often be entirely misplaced, have the opposite of the intended effect. It makes, for instance, a huge difference in reception if a piece of music is performed as part of a festival, on the street, as the background to a TV commercial, or at a children's birthday party. Even if the artist and the delivery of the piece is identical. More significantly, a good performance on stage for a dubious cause might validate the artist's offensive political aims and can be thus, be viewed as harmful propaganda, like 'executing orders' under a repressive regime (Arendt 1951). The film "Mephisto", based on the long-banned novel of the same name by Klaus Mann, illustrates this dilemma brilliantly, showing us the actor-performer as a political puppet. The protagonist of the novel for the film, the manuscript was printed in 1936 in a Parisian magazine, is loosely based on the German actor Gustaf Gründgens, and uses a Faustian 'framework' by having the main character ingratiate himself with the Nazi regime to improve his social position.

This framework takes on particular resonance since the performative activist interventions of the artist Nan Goldin in her ongoing battle with the Sackler family over the controversial art and medical sponsorships of the family via the company Purdue pharmaceuticals. Such sponsorships can themselves be seen to have a performative quality; to act-out an image of the Sackler family at odds with the reality of their medicines' harmful social side-effects, the performance of philanthropy in the real world of stockholder capitalism. In this sense they are a form of 'propaganda', part of a Culture Industry as described by Theodore Adorno, the context makes the difference (Adorno 2001).

A meaningful evaluation simultaneously takes the framework in which the performance is placed and the performance itself. Only with this duality we can begin to evaluate any kind of performance. With this in mind a good performance that synthesises action and framework can deliver results beyond expectation, and sometimes even 'against' expectations. The protagonists as a character of a performance may master all elements that constitute the overall event, the performance as a framework, and takes the result of the performance beyond its expected limits. A good performance holds a lot of power. It has four 'E's': it can engage, entertain, excite, and educate.

Nourished with these powers' performance can be a call to action. It can allow us to create a common ground and a means of togetherness and community, as few other areas of engagement can. As an example of the power of performance in various forms, the authors of this book organised as part of the of the Architectural Association Public Programme, a series of events under the title "Performance, Protest, Politics". During this series distinctive lectures were delivered as 'performance presentations'.

Performance presentation

We define Performance Presentation to underline the argument of the direct power of performance; its effectiveness as means to use 'speech' to cause 'action' (Arendt 1958). Performance as presentation can create an immersive atmosphere that engages an audience and invites it to participate in the discourse, if the content is presented in a way that eschews the usual divide of lecturer and listener, scholar, and student, and instead creates an environment as a shared experience of an event.

The inaugural events of performance presentations for us as a studio were the 2010 "Seed to Scene" series in Covent Garden. These can quite literally be seen as the seeds for the networks and ways of working we utilise at the Interprofessional Studio. We began to think about how we might identify like-minded spirits and overlapping interests; we learned how to distinguish between desired collaborators and synergies from less rigorous or advantage-seeking individuals and groups. These initial events became a testing ground: fertile soil for the seeds we planted, looking to new blooms, new ways of collaborating through overlaps and initiatives. And thus, over the course of the year and during the two-week events in Dryden Street, many collaborators of our core team came together for the first time, bringing with them new kinds of knowledge and innovation.

During that first year the studio started to collaborate with the "Boilerhouse Boys" Ben Wolf and Andy Dean, two Grammy-winning music producers and DJs, inventors and entrepreneurs. Whilst Ben had already created lasting networks with creatives across Europe and the UK, Andy established the ambitious way of setting up multi-disciplinary events within the studio. He can only be described as the 'networker from heaven'. At any given moment, Andy will prioritise active enabling of networks above speculative name-dropping. We asked Andy if he had any ideas for artists who could aid our project. Students asked for a couple of young upcoming musicians and Andy immediately established connections to a few bands that would be able to play a gig at the venue. However, given the venue's restrictions we could not accommodate these in a secure way. Most producers would have given up.

Andy, however, just asked us and the students to describe more carefully what they actually wanted to achieve. The response was captured as a desire to create an interactive environment that bridged the different disciplines in a new, unexpected way. Andy walked out of the room to make a call and returned with the announcement that he could secure David McAlmont, a musical performer with an extensive and cultured group of followers who could add significantly to the kind of conversations we try to create. David went on with us to create an evening based upon interaction and music. It is no overstatement to say that at this night a new modus operandi was established for many of us. He is still using this unique form of genre-defying art and performance by presenting creative culture and art history in lectures and talks whilst contextualising it with his outstanding musical interpretations, and once-in-a-generation voice.

For the entire AAIS team, the events presented in the first season created moments of calm and reflection: we were in the presence of absolute creative professionalism. Here we could see at a glance what it means to be absolutely at the top of your game within your field of art, and at the same time be generous in the collective quest for innovation. Andy's interactive conversation with David embedded in the unusual timber structures surrounding them, created an 'open source' exchange, which became one of the core methodologies of the studio. David's way of mixing historic and anecdotal narratives with conversation became the basis of an approach overlapping into some of his own cultural interests, as he noted at the end of the year.

"Andy Dean was approached by the AAIS to assist with a programme of events for their 'Seed to Scene' salon season in Covent Garden in May. He immediately asked me and Guy, gave my fans free admission, interviewed me on the night and made me feel like a visiting legend. Significantly he asked me to do something 'interactive': that simple request singularly transformed my live shows: suddenly they were no longer about 'Me', but 'Us' and the tears and laughs have been flowing ever since. It was also the birth night of my 'Me & My Peops' albums." David McAlmont (16th Dec 2010 on a Facebook Feed).

4.1
Projection during 2020 lecture series
Performance, Protest Politics at the
Architectural Association in London. (TS)

4.2
First "Performance Presentation" in form of an interactive performance and
conversation between David McAlmont and Andy Dean as part of the Seed
to Scene festival in Covent Garden in 2010. (TH)

4.3
Timber-bark structure constructed
out of off-cuts at the Seed to Scene
festival in Covent Garden. (TH)

Performative Lectures

This approach was developed further in many of the resulting performances of the studio. Their academic and political potential, however, came most clearly into focus during the "Performance, Protest, Politics" lecture series at the Architectural Association in 2019. Performance presentation extends beyond the described shows. A framework of public relations, announcements, documentation, and follow-up is essential to create a lasting after-effect. Here the topics of presentation road-tested a broad field of engagements.

Besides the four writers of this chapter, the Artist and AAIS tutor Argyris Angeli, the art historian, AAIS tutor and singer David McAlmont as well Stephan Trüby the professor for Architecture and Cultural Theory of the University of Stuttgart presented various approaches to the subject. Argyris Angeli presented on forms of collaboration where creation of art through performance, lecture and live logging of the event took place as a hybrid between performative lecture and workshop. David McAlmont together with Pierre Nedd delivered a 'jazzification' on Heracles. The mythological history of Heracles was illustrated as an immersive performance accompanied by newly arranged mixes of jazz legend Duke Ellington, resulting in not only a comprehensive, academic lecture on the subject but probably the first standing ovation the AA's lecture hall has ever seen. The final lecture of the series was the most political. Stephan Trüby delivered a lecture on "Rechte Räume", meaning right-wing spaces, in which he demonstrated the influence of politics, newly re-emerging populist and right-wing politics, found in public spaces (Trüby 2019). The lecture itself started as a protest against fascist architecture.

The Studio founders Theo Lorenz and Tanja Siems created for the "Performance, Protest, Politics" lecture series a common Ground of discourse. Around a 3-course dinner in the AA lecture hall each course was illustrated with the example of an inspiring pair of individuals within the areas around performance, protest, and politics. This duo was animated through an interactive sculpture sitting on both sides of the presenters to create a dialogue between these two mentors and the performer of the lecture. We started the performance presentation with the theme Protest; our chosen mentors for this topic were the pair of Daniel Marc Cohn-Bendit, a decade bridging advocate for sustainable evolvements, and Greta Thunberg the world-wide know climate activist. The pair we selected for the presentation and discussion of ground-breaking performances in relation to art, dance and theatre were Pina Bausch and Kurt Schwitters. The final mentors for the subject Politics are the ambassadorial Pioneers Hannah Arendt and Martin Luther King Jr.

We organised the presentations around a culinary experience, as we believe that any political discussion should begin by creating common ground between as many participants, interested parties, and affected individuals as possible. This common ground, as a starting point, creates mutual understanding and a basis for finding solutions to upcoming tasks. Culinary events as a mediator could create such common grounds as a mediating tool within difficult diplomatic tasks. *"Culinary experiences have proven to be mediating components during the creative process within the project development. A menu developed specifically for the respective situation becomes a performative element that appeals to the senses and can thus connect the different interests of the actors involved"*. As we experienced over the years *"Architecture and creative work requires the ability to combine different ingredients, to create something new that is not just the addition of its parts. To do this, one must know the ingredients and their behaviour, imagine how they work together and complement each other before beginning the creation. The same applies to culinary creations. A recipe is not just about the dish: presentation, atmosphere, budget and company are the main ingredients; all part of the overall experience."* (Lorenz and Siems 2021, p 35-37.)

The spatial arrangement during the culinary experiences and the lecture were always changing. Half of the audience was placed at the perimeter of the performing area in a fixed seating configuration the other half was in the middle seated on a big table which was taken apart in the different sections of the presentation. In this regard it was possible to change the view and the perception during the whole presentation and to situate the presenter as well, either between or in front of the audience. Through these audible and visual changes to the space, as well as the tasting of various foods, we were able to trigger the audience's observation and senses , and thereby enhance the overall experience of the performative presentation.

As important as the food, is to set up the scene of the space to create a safe atmosphere for discussions. Extensive testing was required beforehand to manage and synchronise all the different performative elements of the presentation. Therefore, we created a mock-up space of the lecture hall to create and test the various projection fields for the presentation of the content as images and films for the lecture, as well as the two projectable sculptures and audio areas for the six mentors, and their interaction as pairs. In parallel to the technical and artistic testing trials, we collected and evaluated all the important data for creating the **essential** substance for the performative **presentation.** The sequences of the presentation sections, starting with Protest, followed by Performance and ending with Politics **as the content of the lecture, was important in order to build up the** argument of the scales in which they could unfold and be applied. Following our intense research around the subject of how to progress in Protest as active performances in relation to Politics starting with the pair of Daniel and Greta following up the discussion with Pina and Kurt and ending with Hannah and Martin are relevant to the scale of activism in their own field.

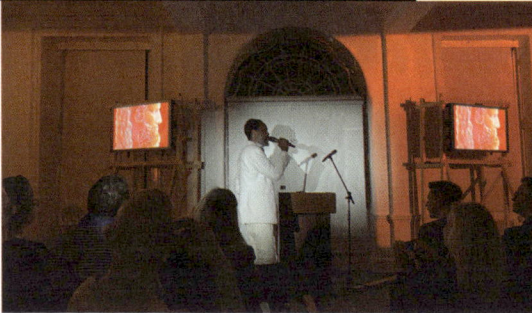

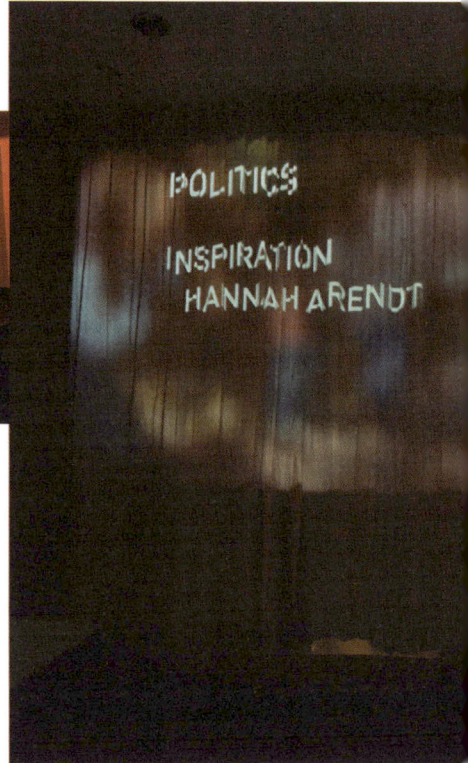

4.4/5
Presentation " I was told to. She asked. We made." By Argyris Angeli with guest participants Jeph Vanger, Caterina Danzico and Nasha Bahasoean as part of the Performance, Protest Politics lecture series at the Architectural association 2020. (TL)

4.6/7
David McAlmont's and Mista Pierre's performance "Heracles: a pictorial jazzification" at the Performance, Protest Politics lecture series 2020. (TS)

4.8
Setup for Tanja Siems's and Theo Lorenz's culinary
performance lecture "Participatory Performance
and After Effect" at the AA lecture hall 2020. (TS)

4.9
Three course dinner by Theo Lorenz and Tanja
Siems as part of the culinary performance lecture
"Participatory Performance and After Effect". (TS)

4.10/11
Tests for interactive setup of
lecture "Participatory Performance
and After Effect". (TS)

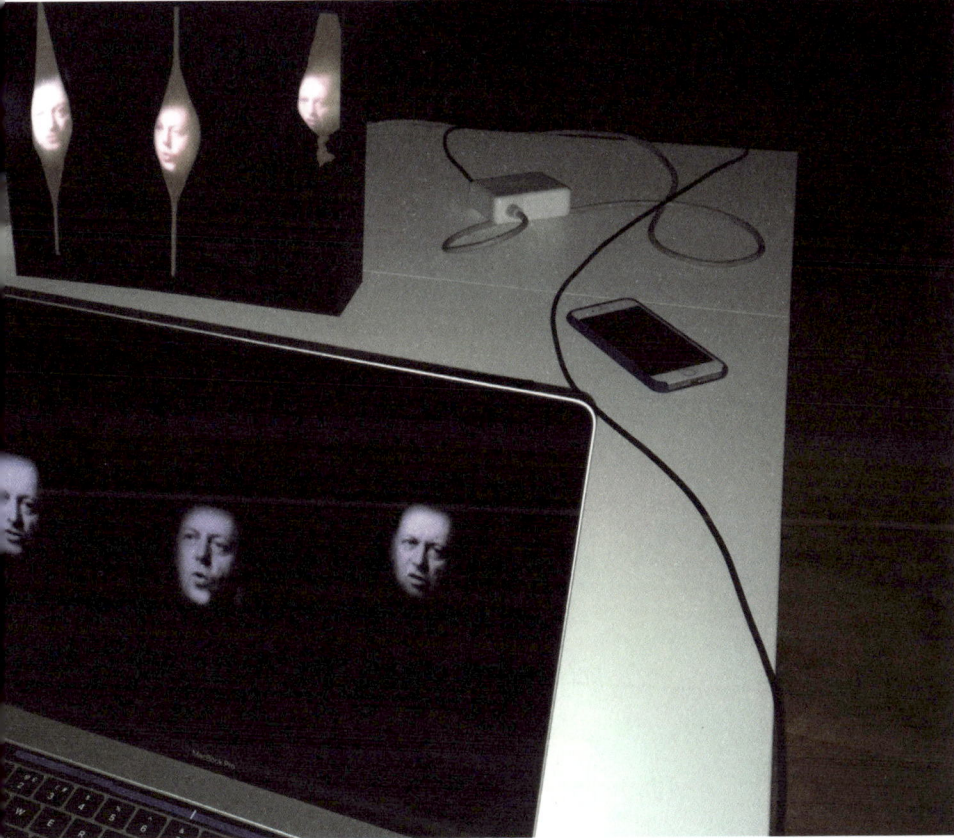

4.12
Preparation for the lecture
"Participatory Performance and After
Effect" with haptic elements. (TL)

At the beginning of each section the theme Protest, Performance or Politics got introduced by the animated mentors, which were projected on the white fabric sculpture, hence they talked and moved in an artistic manner and were 'set back to life'. To fertilise the discussion the spatial arrangement and the changing atmosphere was as important as the ingredients of the plant-based food we created. The room atmosphere changed per sections of the presentation as the overall light changed in parallel with the images which were projected on the main screen. This atmospheric arrangement and the chosen ingredients of the plant-based cuisine set the scene of each 'chapter' which was experienced by the audience in parallel to the content presentations.

In the follow-up lecture Portia Kamons, an American producer, gave a detailed performance presentation about a series of creative acts of performative protest which confront urgent social issues of their time and framework. Because she has personal relationships with all five of the case studies she presented, she *performed* a personal history of politics and performance. The talk was made in front of a screen which covered the entire length of the AA's lecture hall, featuring with one continuous projection, giving the impression of a news studio. *"I used to think art was dumb and had no real purpose, only to realise over the past five years art and storytelling are the two most"* (Hogg 2022).

Portia began by asking: *"Can we all agree, in principle if not down to granular detail, that our presence in this room, at this institution of the AA, with these people in this city at this time in history is enough to qualify us as among the most privileged people on our planet. We have water, food, shelter and beyond that, access. To education, to opportunity, to powerful networks of people who are sitting beside you in this lecture hall or your classrooms, or in the cinema or on the tube or on your social media feeds. You never know. Cities fizz with the energy from these human networks, even if they haven't been fully activated yet. They fizz with potential. Of course, the opposite of this is also true: elsewhere on our planet are people who struggle daily to find food, water, shelter, healthcare, education, peace, opportunity or safety. So, I think it's reasonable to ask: what are we going to do with our privilege? What stories will you tell the children of the future about what we did with our time now? Because I think they're going to want to know."* This position was her framework.

Case studies of political activism

Portia's first case study considered the political activism that emerged in New York in response to the AIDS crisis of the 1980s and 1990s. Between 1987 and 1991, the AIDS epidemic claimed the lives of over 150,000 people in the United States alone. At that point in time there was no treatment, no cure, and no end in sight. Portia introduced clips form Jean Carlomusto's 2015 film, "Larry Kramer in Love and Anger", we met Larry as he addresses an AIDS forum in New York City. *"Larry was a writer. He had no medical training, no political experience, no history of activism. But he stepped into the breech and led the fight. He co-founded the Gay Men's Health Crisis (GMHC) and formed ActUP– the AIDS Coalition to Unleash Power, a direct-action protest group agitating ferociously, relentlessly, dramatically and creatively for solutions to the AIDS crisis."* Throughout the era Jean Carlomusto, a filmmaker and documentarian, gathered footage of Kramer's activism *by being there*. She attended the meetings, developed relationships with the key players, recorded the history, and had the presence of mind to archive everything. "Larry Kramer in Love and Anger" was nominated for the Grand Jury Prize when it premiered at the Sundance Film Festival in 2015. It was distributed by HBO, and received two Emmy nominations. *"I asked Jean what alerted her to the need to shoot and preserve this footage? And what sustained, and kept her working on it over the following decades? She answered: 'I made the film to show how the persistent agitation on the part of one person could inspire a movement to fight back against all odds and create lasting change.'"*

What does the film mean twenty and sometimes thirty years after the events they present? In 2015 the framework is in a world of very different political activism. A screening may well be new history to some in an audience, their response in discussion afterwards informed by discussions which consider other kinds of politics.

Another theatrical work which embodied the red-hot-rage, confusion and death-defying exuberance of the early AIDS era was a show called "Father Was a Peculiar Man", produced in 1991 by En Garde Arts, where Portia worked as a producer. It was one of the very first examples of site-specific theatre to take place in New York. The show was conceived and directed by Reza Abdoh and was commissioned to take place in 14 different locations throughout the meatpacking district in lower Manhattan.

4.13/14
"Participatory Performance and
After Effect" by Theo Lorenz and
Tanja Siems. (TS)

4.15
Theo Lorenz introducing Portia Kamons for her performance
lecture "Acting Up" as part of the lecture series Performance,
Protest Politics at the Architectural Association. (TS)

4.16
Theo Lorenz introducing Portia Kamons for her performance lecture "Acting Up" as part of the
lecture series Performance, Protest Politics at the Architectural Association. (TS) Portia Kamons
presenting "Father Was a Peculiar Man" a verbatim theatre projects during her lecture. (TS)

En Garde Arts was the first theatre company in New York devoted exclusively to commissioning new performance works that used the city itself as its stage. Founder Annie Hamburger, a visionary theatre producer who believed, then and now, in the power of theatrical performance to challenge the status quo, turn it on its head, and make an impact. "Father Was a Peculiar Man" remains one of the most consequential works in En Garde's 35-year history. If you've been to New York in the 21st Century, you'll know that the meatpacking district is now home to the Whitney Museum and the very chic High Line. But in 1991, the neighbourhood was relatively unknown to most New Yorkers. It was dark, dirty, dangerous, deeply territorial. It was common to see bloody animal carcasses in the streets of the wholesale meat market by day, and another kind of meat market by night, populated by transvestite sex workers, their customers, pimps, also after hour sex-clubs and a veritable night market selling drugs.

There were some scrapes, by day and by night. The negotiating of permissions from property owners to access power lines and hang scenery from the 19th century buildings. At first everyone refused, one tough guy stopped the En Garde team cold, mid-pitch and said *"Get outta my office."* When they cheerfully persisted, he pulled his jacket back, revealed his pistol and repeated, *"get OUTTA MY OFFICE."* But eventually finally they found their way to the neighbourhood's Boss, Jim Ortensio of Long Island Beef.

> *"And, when I told him my name was Portia, he recited the entire soliloquy from the Merchant of Venice in his mobster accent: 'The quality of Mercy is not strained…it dropeth like the gentle rain from heaven….' And that was that. Jim gave us the keys to the kingdom. And we gave Reza this extraordinary palette to unleash his imagination onto."*

En Garde Arts built a 120-foot-long dining table with a chandelier and giant meat cleaver suspended overhead. There was a graveyard, and a Prairie Homestead and a 60-foot-high curtain suspended from the Westside Highway where they simulated a *hanging* every night from the railway trestle that is now the luxuriant High Line. Inside a blood-stained meat locker, they built a nightmarish winter wonderland and S&M sex dungeon. It wasn't always possible to tell the difference between actor and audience, scenery and cityscape, sacred or profane. It was mad. It was a physical manifestation of the AIDS nightmare.

> The New York Times wrote: *"Near the beginning of 'Father Was a Peculiar Man', an exhilarating evening of environmental street theatre presented by En Garde Arts, an actor from the company of more than 60 performers approaches the audience and excitedly offers his theory on the significance of (the pop star) Madonna. By suggesting that sex is possible in the age of AIDS, he says, she is 'Trying to become a Christ. She will link us together'"* (Holden 1990).

Madonna didn't feature in the show. But Jesus did. And the Kennedys and Marilyn Monroe among a cast of 60 performers. And a giant beanstalk, a marching band, a red Cadillac convertible, and the trans sex-workers who were working the streets each night. Every member of the audience became part of the show as well, which is why people who were there still remember it to this day.

> *"There was medicine before Larry Kramer, and medicine after Larry Kramer"*
> Anthony Fauci, American immunologist.

Portia's third case study, "Basetrack", was the most labyrinthine of the projects presented. The photographer Teru Kuwayama had between 2009 and 2013 travelled independently, meaning without the cover provided by sponsorship of a news organisation, with three collaborators to the Gulf states and southern Afghanistan to chronicle the day-to-day experiences of the 1stbatallion/8thdivision of the US Marine Corps. Their images convey granular, personal and gut-wrenching details of the Gulf War experience that most people would never get a chance to see. When traditional media outlets declined to publish their work, Teru and his team created an experimental media project called "Basetrack".

The idea was deceptively simple. They used Facebook to publish the photos and in doing so connected the Marines with their friends and families back home. In a remarkably short period of time the page attracted millions of users: at its peak five million. Perhaps inevitably, the US Department of Defense tried to shut the site down –after all the posts included details that could reveal their locations and activities – but after an outcry from military families "Basetrack" was allowed to stay online.

The result of this experiment is an archive of strangely beautiful, complex, unsanitised images that are a window opening to reveal the impact of war on both the Afghan people and the American Marines. As Kuwayama puts it, *"Nobody has more authenticity [than the Marines] to talk about this war, its costs, its consequences, and maybe even offer some analysis about how this could be done better."*

Edward Bilous, an award-winning composer, producer and the founding director of the Center for Innovation in the Arts at the Juilliard School in New York City came across an exhibition of the photos by Teru at a gallery in New York City. He commissioned a playwright and multi-media designer; worked with En Garde to produce "Basetrack", the theatrical performance which debuted at the Brooklyn Academy of Music to rave reviews in 2014.

It's hard to imagine three less likely people to tackle a narrative about US Marines than Annie, Ed and Portia. Every member of the collaborative team opposed the Gulf Wars. None had military experience, or any interest in the American military machine. What they did have was a genuine concern for the suffering of veterans and their families. A historically large number of soldiers from the Gulf Wars survived terrible injuries and returned home with profound disabilities, physical as well as psychological. Once they left the military, these vets and their families were very often isolated in communities where people didn't yet understand the effects or even the symptoms of PTSD. When the project began, twenty-two American veterans were committing suicide every day. This was making a huge impact on communities across the United States. There was already a lot of support for vets with physical injuries, but the team needed to understand how to help the invisible, psychological injuries. Compounding the problem was a very evident, entrenched stigma in military communities around approaching the subject of mental health or, worse, accepting the need for therapy.

So that's where the team focussed its energy. The first thing it did was to assemble an advisory committee of experts in the field of veterans' mental health who advised on every step of the process of creating a performance, with sound, image, spoken word, music and acting. None of what followed could have happened without this panel. The team realised it couldn't simply impose a narrational framework on Teru's images. Instead, they identified Marines in the photographs, contacted them through Facebook, and conducted over 100 hours of interviews with the members of the First Battalion/the Eighth Marines, the 1/8 as they're known, and their families. Playwright Jason Grote used this to construct a script made up solely of verbatim text. The story centring on a Marine named A.J. Czubai, and his wife Melissa. Jason ordered the text into a story arc that chronicled their early life together, A.J.'s enlistment, deployment, and homecoming.

But he didn't change a single syllable
from the recorded interviews.

Using verbatim text prevented the team from embellishing the stories for dramatic effect. It also prevented the shying away from the harshest truth of the soldier's experiences. Most of all, the creative team hoped this rigour in performance and framework would give the work a degree of authenticity that transcended a fictional account. They cast a Marine, Tyler LaMarr, in the role of AJ. To differentiate between our project and Teru's ongoing experiment we called the show "Basetrack Live". When "Basetrack Live" opened, The New York Times wrote: *"The experience of soldiers fighting the long wars in Iraq and Afghanistan have been widely documented, of course, but Basetrack Live brings a vital intimacy, and a compelling visual allure, to the journalistic enterprise. Most of us know about the impact of the wars on the soldiers, including numerous suicides, but this production brings the gritty, brutal truths alive in ways that nothing I've read or seen has succeeded in doing"* (Isherwood 2014).

The Times included "Basetrack Live" in the top ten productions of the year. After this, the show was toured across the country. It played at theatres, but also universities, community centres, and military bases. And at every show, in New York City and around the country, the team worked very hard to make sure the audience included veterans and their families. Every night after each performance they hosted events that gave people a rare opportunity to talk about the mental health issues raised in the show. Tyler would ask any Vets in the audience to stand: they always got a round of applause. Then he asked people to raise their hands if they knew someone now serving in the military. Then if they knew someone who served in historical conflicts. Eventually more than half the audience had their hands raised. For the next 30 minutes, the team asked questions that facilitated a dialogue between these two very different constituencies. It was profoundly moving. One of the advisory committee members unexpectedly convinced the Army to conduct a study on combat vets who attended a show. They identified a 36% reduction in the stigma associated with seeking therapeutic help after seeing a production of "Basetrack Live". Which everyone found astonishing.

"Basetrack Live" was a genuinely radical experiment, an eye-opening experience for everyone involved. It broke down some of the barriers which exist between veterans and civilians in the United States. Over 40,000 people were killed by guns in the United States in 2022 and the figures have been distressingly high for decades. When composer Ron Ramin invited Portia Kamons to collaborate on a project addressing the youth activism which erupted after the Parkland shootings of 2018 there was an opportunity to expand on the idea of transforming verbatim interviews into documentary performance. "Seventeen" is a work in progress and debuted in Orlando in November 2024.

The relentless torrent of news about gun violence in America is, of course, heart-breaking. But it met a tipping point on 14th February 2018 when a gunman killed 17 people at Marjorie Stoneman Douglas School in Parkland, Florida. Just six weeks into the year, it was already the 10th mass school shooting. This time, the usual 'thoughts and prayers' met with the molten rage of a generation of kids who had had enough. Within weeks youth-led activism in southern Florida exploded across the state and the country. The students demanded to be heard. The empty chairs in their classrooms which belonged to best friends brutally lost would fuel their fight for rest of their lives.

They were smart. They listened. They understood the long-simmering despair in black and brown communities that had already given rise to the "Black Lives Matter" movement. They went to Chicago to meet with the young people there who'd been fighting against epic, entrenched gun violence for generations. The Chicago kids went to Florida to hang out together and figure out a strategy. Within weeks, there was a national school walkout, and a national die-in day. They descended on their state legislatures.

When all they got for the initial campaigning was more 'thoughts and prayers', they organised in a matter of weeks the "March for Our Lives". The march was America's biggest youth-led protest since the Vietnam War. An estimated 800,000 people filled the streets of Washington, DC and many millions more gathered on every continent around the world. They marched. They made demands. They started running for political office. And then they finished High School.

"Seventeen" is not a top-down teaching by boomer educators, but a recognition of the energy, passion and vision of young people bring to the public forum as they rise toward fully adult human potency, bringing invention and creativity to existing norms and practices, typically without any help from other generations with other ways of seeing. Perhaps a generation which saw the Black Lives Matter movement corrupted to rapidly by the "Blue Lives" and "All Lives Matter" movements, created seemingly by activists whose sole mission was to dissipate the massive impact of "Black Lives Matter".

Ron Ramin is a classical composer. With Portia Kamons he is developing a multimedia work for symphony orchestra which amplifies the young activists driving this movement. It started by following these activists on social media, and then, just as with the processes of "Basetrack Live", recording interviews which have been used to build a libretto, which is once again exclusively verbatim. The multimedia projection design is made from artefacts collected from the activists' own photographs and social media feeds, together with online and offline news sources.

"Seventeen" has highlighted a significant issue about performance and politics, which is the impact of time on the frameworks and prisms through which a work is approached. The truth is these kids mean business and have made a phenomenal impact immediately. They don't really need help getting their message across. However, the older, conservative-skewing audience for symphony orchestras is a crucial target constituency for those who want to see meaningful gun reform in America. The classical music demographic is very likely to fall outside the reach of existing teenage social networks. So, seven years after the Parkland shootings the hope with "Seventeen" is to take the conversation that has taken place on the streets and online to the more rarefied acoustics of the concert hall.

Protest:

Protest can have many forms and scales. It is fundamentally an expression of disapproval and a critique of a situation or circumstance. Protest all too often is framed as destructive, an unwanted interruption of the norm. However, in the context of performance and politics, protest can be seen as a platform and means of dialogue to create common ground.

It is important to distinguish the direction and dynamic this process can take. We distinguish between three major directions of protest: destructive, preservative, and creative.

A destructive form of protest is 'against' something. It often aims to destroy or overturn an existing condition. It might be a form of protest that could spiral into violence. A preservative protest, however, aims to maintain a condition that may be in danger of being changed or challenged. This may be a positive or a negative outcome and is probably the most likely to be misinterpreted. A creative protest, meanwhile, tries to build and extend ideas, whilst challenging the prevailing conditions.

These basic forms of protest are not discrete and all too often transform from one to the other. We all are familiar with Jacques Mallet du Pan's expression that *"The Revolution devours its children"* as a reaction to the aftermath of the French Revolution (Mallet du Pan 1793).

A creative idea might trigger a destructive outcome and in turn cause a reactionary desire for preservation. A fear of loss and the wish to preserve a given situation might turn into a violent and defensive uprising that in its devastation could drive the need for new and creative solutions to overcome the situation. A need of preservation and protection might lead to creative ideas that if not successful still might lead to elements of destruction. The cycles and interactions of performance and framework are infinitely nuanced.

The primary aim of protest in relation to our ideas of performance and politics is to create positive after-effects by creating a common ground. We believe creative protest should not be merely 'against' something but also be 'for' something. However, we also believe that protest needs to be a compassionate reaction to the world around us, advocating mutual understanding and leading to creative innovation.

'Stepping Up' And 'Stepping In'

To achieve these positive goals, we think that any creative protest should have as a base premise the idea of 'stepping up' and taking responsibility for the topic being addressed. It is not enough to point at something, but it is necessary to use the creative platform to actively change the thinking about a given situation. It is important to distinguish here between 'stepping up' and 'stepping in'. 'Stepping up' means the taking of responsibility within a network or collective. It is an act of supporting a process so that its movement can go forward and unfold in a coherent, traceable, and documentable way. 'Stepping in', on the other hand, can mean that a process has failed; the situation requires intervention. The first is a form of responsible collaboration; the second is a form of top-down hierarchy.

4.17
Portia Kamons presenting US Marine
Corps Gulf War experiences through
art during her lecture "Acting Up". (TS)

4.18
Discussion between Portia Kamons and Madeleine
Kate McGowan about the project "Other Story"
as part of the "acting up" lecture. (TS)

4.19
Portia Kamons presenting the seventeen project
and protest project "the March for Our Lives"
in reaction to gun violence in the US. (TS)

To return to the streets from the concert hall an interesting reference point as we consider the development of forms of protest into forms of art and applied methodologies might be the movement around the Situationist (Debord 1958). The movement in relation to the widespread protests against the political establishment of the post-war de Gaulle government around the Sorbonne University in the 1950s and1960s formulated ways of understanding the city as an active act (Debord 1967) reading the urban landscape through psycho-geographical maps. This process of (apparent) random drifting in order to find new potentials, to unfold situations, is both performative and reliant on frameworks generated by political or social, or individuated, goals. The methodology of wandering around a city without a given destination was intended to help residents experience their living quarters in new ways. It built on work which grew out the literatures of nineteenth century France, and the performative gestural politics of Dada in early post-First World War France.

Guy Debord demonstrates once again that the familiar urban corner can provide a myriad of surprises through a different view and a different frame of the structures and the individual passers-by. In his psycho-geographical mapping the 'Naked City', he tries to log the everyday life of Paris in a creative cartography. In his artistic approach of the map, he tried to split the city into individual parts and to bring together the situations experienced whilst strolling into new kinds of sequences. The theory of the Situationists International and their artistic approach was subsequently used as a tool of performative protest against the establishment of the Sorbonne University with various activists inside and outside the university.

We at the studio feel it is vital that political and social protest is reflected and expressed in artistic actions, in performance based on radical truths. A radical approach to protest through aggressive and violent behaviour is neither efficient or progressive, nor particularly meaningful. Violence usually leads to further violence, revolutions to terrors, unfocused disputes with an executive can be effective in the short-term for press or social media relations but is not constructive as a sustainable protest movement continuing the progress of important critical activism.

Politics:

If we talk about politics, we at the studio do not talk about a top-down form of governing based on *party*, but rather about the processes of negotiation which are possible between equals in relation to a shared social situation or situations. Within this framework politics become a collection of dynamic tools to search, discuss, negotiate, and ultimately create solutions. In this way politics is no longer defined as governance of the existing. It is rather the act of recognising imbalance of our framework and seeking through aligned performance/framework the necessary developments that result in progressive works and efforts to bring about change for the better. This requires persistence. Persistence sometimes against impossible odds. This form of politics can be situated in any scale, and process of creation. It is a positive attitude towards building, transforming and changing. It is often based on strong tools of analysis and research. It is a process that is the fundament of togetherness and thus underlying education. It is a process underlying design.

The basis of politics in performance and design is found in the work of Hannah Arendt, most prominently in her book "The Human Condition" (Arendt 1958). Here she sees politics as an active participation in the processes that form the society around us, taking part not merely hypothetically, and thus remaining in a 'vita completiva', but also actively forming, creating, contributing, and enriching the world around us as individuals. Arendt's 'vita activa' enables us to develop the world around us and live as free beings in an attempt to avoid a top-down governance of restrictions. Participation in creation, participation in design, and participation in performance enable us to constantly transform thought into realities, to build frameworks that allow for the continuous unfolding of ideas and realisations which can overcome artificial external limitations and bureaucratic restrictions.

Our studio's goal in our studies and presentations is to further a contemporary 'vita activa' which can help to overcome a 'vita bureaucratia', a limiting system that enables and empowers the mindless execution of given directives or orders without contemplating their effect or usefulness. This definition of politics is creative and inspiring we believe. It does not look for idols or leaders, but for initiatives, participations, and for the taking of responsibility. A politics that is not passive and requires its participants to engage in activity. A politics which is knowledgeable about all its parts, performance and framework, subject, and object, and is transparent to innovation and development. Performance, art, and design can be seen as crucial tools in the formation of a progressive common ground, tools which allow performers to stay active and involved continuously; to create public spaces that make where a principle of initiative and possibility can occur. Creativity, one might say, is the action that allows one to move dynamically through the distinct areas of the 'vita activa': labour, work, and action, guided by thought informed by both performance and framework

References

Acconci, Vito (1969) Following Piece. Performance. New York City.
Adorno, Theodor W. (2001) The Culture Industry: Enlightenment as Mass Deception. 2nd edn. London: Routledge.
Arendt, Hannah (1951) The Origins of Totalitarianism. New York: Schocken Books.
Arendt, Hannah (1958) The Human Condition. Chicago: University of Chicago Press.
Breton, André (1999 [1928]) Nadja. London: Penguin Modern Classics.
Debord, Guy E. (1958) Internationale situationniste, no. 1. Paris: Editorial Committee Mohamed Dahou, Giuseppe Pinot Gallizio, Maurice Wyckaert.
Debord, Guy E. (1967) La société du spectacle. Translated as Society of the Spectacle (1970). Detroit: Black & Red.
Goldin, Nan (2018) 'I survived the opioid crisis', Artforum.
Graeber, David (2018) Bullshit Jobs. New York: Simon & Schuster.
Hogg, David (2022) 'I used to think art was dumb and had no real purpose...', Twitter, 18 September, 11:03 PM. Available at: https://x.com/davidhogg111 (Accessed: 2025).
Holden, Stephen (1990) 'Review/Theater; A Carnival of Satire and Savagery, With a Karamazov as Ringmaster', The New York Times, 11 July. Available at: https://www.nytimes.com/1990/07/11/theater/review-theater-a-carnival-of-satire-and-savagery-with-a-karamazov-as-ringmaster.html (Accessed: 2025).

Isherwood, Charles (2014) 'Lives of Returning Marines in Basetrack Live at BAM', The New York Times, 12 November. Available at: https://www.nytimes.com/2014/11/13/theater/lives-of-returning-marines-in-basetrack-live-at-bam.html(Accessed: 2025).
Lorenz, Daniela and Siems, Thomas (2021) 'Cooking up Ideas – Culinary Interventions', in Food and the City as Planning Fields of Action. SRL: Association for Urban, Regional and State Planning.
Mallet du Pan, Jacques (1793) Considerations on the Nature of the French Revolution: and on the Causes Which Prolong Its Duration. London: J. Owen.
Mann, Klaus (1995 [1936]) Mephisto. London: Penguin Books.
Plato (2007 [380 BCE]) The Republic. London: Penguin Classics.
Richter, Hans and Britt, David (1978) Dada: Art and Anti-Art. London: Thames & Hudson.
Tate Gallery (2024) Sophie Calle: Artist Biography. Tate Modern. Available at: https://www.tate.org.uk/art/artists/sophie-calle-2692 (Accessed: 2025).
Trüby, Stephan (2019) 'Rechte Räume', ARCH+ Magazine, Berlin.

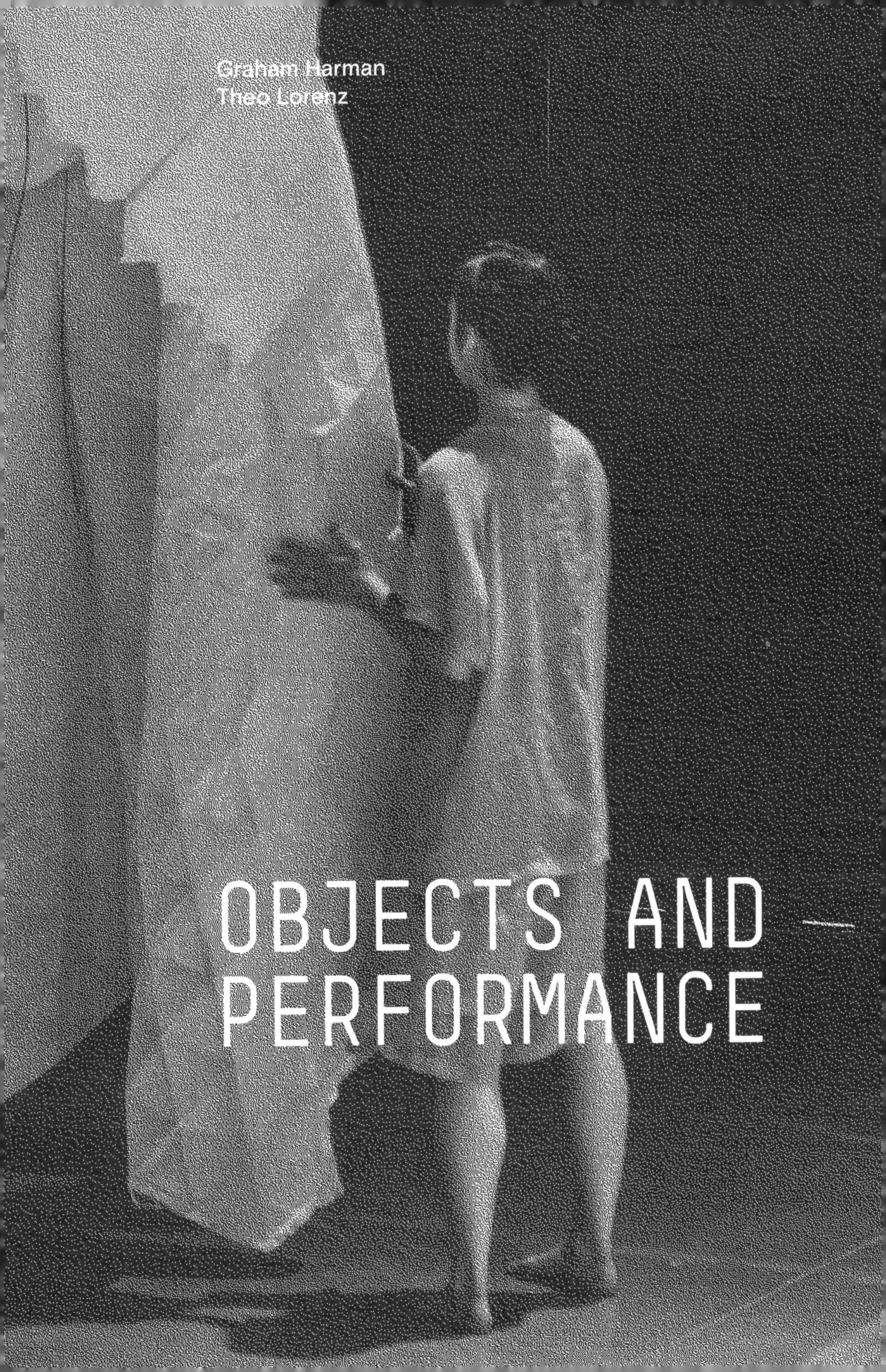

Graham Harman
Theo Lorenz

OBJECTS AND
PERFORMANCE

Objects are always performing. It does not matter if we designed them to fulfil a certain function, or if we look at them whilst they do so; they just perform. Engineers will first consider the performance of any object that is part of their range of concerns. Under what circumstances does the object perform: how, in relation to what, and within what set of goals? This performance occurs on multiple levels simultaneously. Movement, durability, time, expression and even dramaturgy are always present in any object. From the 'swinging Berta' bridge to a simple piece of gravel in the sun, we can both see and interpret all of these elements.

Yet in the context of the performing arts, the performance of the objects themselves might be under-represented at times, or even overlooked. If the objects in question are merely viewed as add-ons, or as decor with limited agency within a performance, the attention to their selection and design might be neglected in such a way as to lead to a result that is overall imbalanced. The agency that objects, props and sets hold within a spatial performance depend on their quality of design.

The quality of their performance, however, does not depend on their beholder and her taste, entertainment, or impression, but on the interplay of all the elements in the performance. An example of a performance that occurs without an audience is the "Moving Stone" project of the Interprofessional Studio in 2015. Set in the remote Gallery of Maniga Barche on Sardinia, the event itself was a serendipitous interplay of elements coming together at a single moment in time to form the overall performance. The Gallery is a roofless, semi-derelict building on the edge of the ocean in Calasetta and is always exposed to the elements. The student design consists of a set of 30 pendula in a grid, set out to react to the elements of wind and sun to form the basis of a narrative and choreography in which the performers react to the movement of the pendula. Under normal weather conditions this would have been, on its own, an interesting interplay of objects and subjects. However, the performance developed into a truly unique event in time at the moment when it took place. For as it happened, a set of natural phenomena intersected and took over. A rare total solar eclipse took place on March 20th, changing the entirety of the atmosphere on nothing less than a cosmic scale. Simultaneously, hurricane-force winds arose on Sardinia. The objects of the set thus became dramatic actants highlighting these unique natural occurrences. The performers, the dancer Joe Walkling and the singer David McAlmont, needed to subscribe to the directing of the pendula within an accentuated environment. Movement and song were submerged within the power of the objects. The moment in its entirety was neither un-graspable nor documentable and could only be understood through the overlap of all accounts of its parts.

The relation of object and performance can be described in a multitude of ways, according to various scales and dimensions. Yet these two terms must not be conceived as objects. It is customary to speak of art from the 1960s as somehow moving 'beyond the object' toward something with a more event-like character (Rose 1975). Yet for every effort to refer for instance to photography as an 'objectless art' there is the contrary observation that a photograph is the best means of converting an event into an object (Sayre 1983, Garcia 2016). In any case, whether we focus on spatial performance and design or on the performing arts instead, this ranges across a spectrum of objects ranging from site and venue to prop, set, costumes, words, lighting, and physical movement. Yet even an entire performance can be treated as an object. It might be asked: why this inflation of the word 'object', which is normally used to refer only to durable, mid-sized physical solids, or as a foil for its opposite word 'subject', that prince of modern philosophy? To speak of objects allows us to focus on at least two important points. First, it signifies that which has an autonomous or independent character that both resists and moulds our own wishes. In this respect, the object is filled with surprises and exceeds both all possible experience of it and the sum total of discoveries that can be made about it. In this way the object embodies what Jean Baudrillard calls 'the revenge of the crystal': it seduces the subject, whose purported freedom and transcendence are seldom its most relevant features (Baudrillard 1991, Baudrillard 2008). Second, to speak of something as an object implies a durable core of objecthood that persists through its numerous shifting costumes and facial expressions. In recent decades everyone has preferred to speak of 'events', as if transient encounters were the only thing of importance. If we now speak instead of objects, it is to emphasise the ability of things to change their appearance and mood through a vast range of possibilities without losing their identity, which is never fully expressed in any of its encounters. Yet it must also be remembered that far from excluding composition or relationality, the object actually requires them. Consider a simple example such as water, which acts as a unified thing, but upon closer inspection turns out to be a composite made of hydrogen and oxygen in fixed proportion. The fact that water is not as simple, irreducible, and indestructible as believed by the pre-Socratic thinker Thales of Miletus does not mean that water is not an object. This is worth mentioning due to an analogous case of greater importance in the sphere of aesthetics, which one of us has considered elsewhere in some detail (Harman 2020). Immanuel Kant is generally, and rightly, considered to have provided the basis for aesthetic formalism in his *Critique of Judgment* (Kant 1987). For Kant, an artwork should be regarded as cut off both from any conceptual paraphrase of it, and from any merely personal likes or dislikes one has toward its subject matter. The role of the beholders of an artwork is to view it with disinterest, subtracting themselves from it as much as possible, as if the object in question were the physical artwork free of human contamination aside from the minimal act of glancing at it. The prominent critic Michael Fried pursues this way of thinking when he asks us to follow Denis Diderot and oppose any 'theatrical' element in art (Fried 1988). Nonetheless, Fried later acknowledged that in the later course of French painting, the exact opposite occurred. Gustave Courbet painted himself into his own canvases, and Édouard Manet eventually launched modernism by means of pictorial figures who stare at us directly: leading to a 'facingness' in which beholder and artwork become deeply entangled with one another (Fried 1990, Fried 1996). To summarise, the Kantian sort of formalist purity is shown to be impossible. Instead of aesthetics being a matter of a non-human artwork opposed by a human beholder taking great pains not to get too involved, the topic of art turns out to be the composite made of the beholder and the (usually physical) work, just as hydrology is concerned with water as a whole rather than with hydrogen or oxygen in isolation from each other. Contra the early Fried, art is inherently theatrical; all art is performance art. This does not mean that visual art involving human movement or conceptual intervention is somehow privileged over still-life paintings, only that it cannot be excluded from the sphere of high art as high formalism wished.

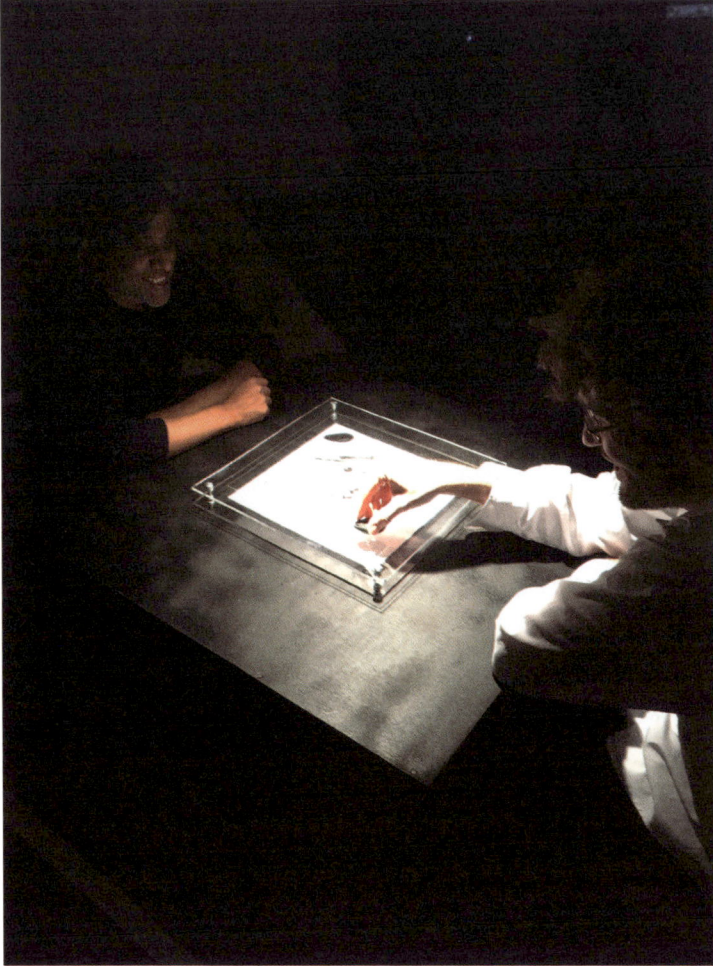

5.1
Gravel on playboard as
choreographic object
triggering movement
of dancers. (DK)

5.2/3
Pendulum outside the Mangia
Barche Gallery on Sardinia in
daylight and the dark during
the solar Eclipse 2015. (DK)

5.4/5
Performance of David McAlmont and Joe
Walkling with a set of pendular objects as
part of "Moving Stone" at the Mangia Barche
Gallery on Calasetta on Sardinia. (DK)

Architecture, Design and Performance
We are often asked what performance has to do with architecture. The word architecture, deriving from the word 'architectus' (meaning 'master builder') implies a discipline concerned with man-made objects. Etymologically speaking, performance refers to 'that which is accomplished'. This intrinsically applied aspect of performance design makes it the ideal testing ground for an architecture that is all too often both hypothetical and slow. A performance is always 'proven by evidence', as it is only existent once it has been delivered. This need for delivery in performance demands initiative, ingenuity, creativity, design, negotiation, teamwork, collaboration and cross-disciplinarity, direction and rehearsal, as well as alterations and even timing, budgeting, fundraising, public relations, and networking. If any of those aspects fail, there is no performance. A performance in its entirety is a realised architecture that embeds in itself the relation between subjects and objects in real-time: delivered and realised, yet open for critique, alterations and further development and contextualisation. What we look for in architecture is qualities.

In a performative approach, the vision of a project is in most cases set less by an 'a priori' idea of a physical manifestation of artefacts. Performative projects are driven from the outset by process. One element builds on the other in a constant exchange. The starting point, the inspiration, can provide a vast variety of options. It might be as different as a narrative, a social or political aim, a piece of art, a specific environment, or a set of movements. This starting-point will call all other elements into the process to drive the overall aim forward. In this way, by default, no element emerges in isolation and on its own. Each element, whether subject or object, develops and transforms in relation to the other. Neglect of any of the elements will be plainly visible in the result, as the weak link within the ensemble. These are the components that critiques will spot immediately. They will be able to highlight if the project contains bad writing or insufficient lighting, if it disregards audience interaction or movement, or if the set and objects fail to aid the overall message of the piece. The design of an object within this setting will, by default, develop as a response to initiative, dialogue, chance, and opportune occurrences, but also through fixed or emergent limitations and restrictions.

The applied testing ground of performance design allows us to reassess seemingly established norms in architecture and design. In performance, the previous set of aims are extended or altered in terms of their position with respect to the subject-object relation. What seems to be a 'best practice' might no longer hold if new criteria are applied. Dancers, for example, look at objects in completely different ways. They don't see them as backgrounds, walls, or props, but rather as elements of their movement. They do not look at the object as an external design, but as an element that either prohibits or enables their performance. In this way, their behaviour towards and with objects is completely different from what we find in day-to-day use. In turn, this extended view might bring new ideas and innovations to the requirements of architecture.

In our first collaboration with choreographers and dancers we discovered new ways of looking at architecture and objects. For the project "Seed to Scene," which took place as a two-week festival in a derelict building in Covent Garden, we came into contact with a group of young choreographers and dancers. From the first moment it was clear that they were after something more than conventional dance approaches. They were not just looking for a new platform; instead, they came as a group, genuinely interested in exchange and discovery based on the specific material and location of the project. Perhaps even more significantly, they wished to interact among themselves as a group of peers. We discussed from the outset how space, design, materiality, and audience could be explored through movement, by creating new transformative connections between all of them. The group, consisting entirely of established and award-winning dancers – Patricia Okenwa, Renaud Wiser, Jonathan Goddard, Joe Walkling, Gemma Nixon, and Clara Barbera – created, together with the students, an approach to the design and space that was utterly immersed within all of the relevant components. Based on fragments of previous choreographic work, they created a site- and network-specific performance that enabled a single fluid experience between the architecture, audience, and performers, breaking down the barriers between them.

This became vividly evident during the performance itself. There was at all times a closeness and relation between performance, audience and space that moved everyone outside of the expected, outside of anyone's comfort zone. The performers interacted with the audience, the audience with the space and design, and the design with the performance. This manner of immersive boundary-less events became not only the trademark of the Interprofessional Studio far beyond dance but also of the unique approach of the New Movement Collective. However, the most remarkable aspect of this new collaboration was a changed attitude towards the objects of design within the set. The prominent design of undulating timber walls that formed its centre was no longer seen as a set of solid structures. Instead, the walls became fluent dance partners of the movement, embracing, lifting, or rejecting the performer. Whereas within the performance this relation was choreographed and designed, it extended further to the audience during and after the performance. The walls were no longer just looked upon as distant artefacts but were explored in their dynamic materiality. Audience members began to embrace and interact with the structures in a way one would not expect in an 'architectural' environment or an exhibition setting. Choreography became the transformative link between subject and object beyond the planned performance itself.

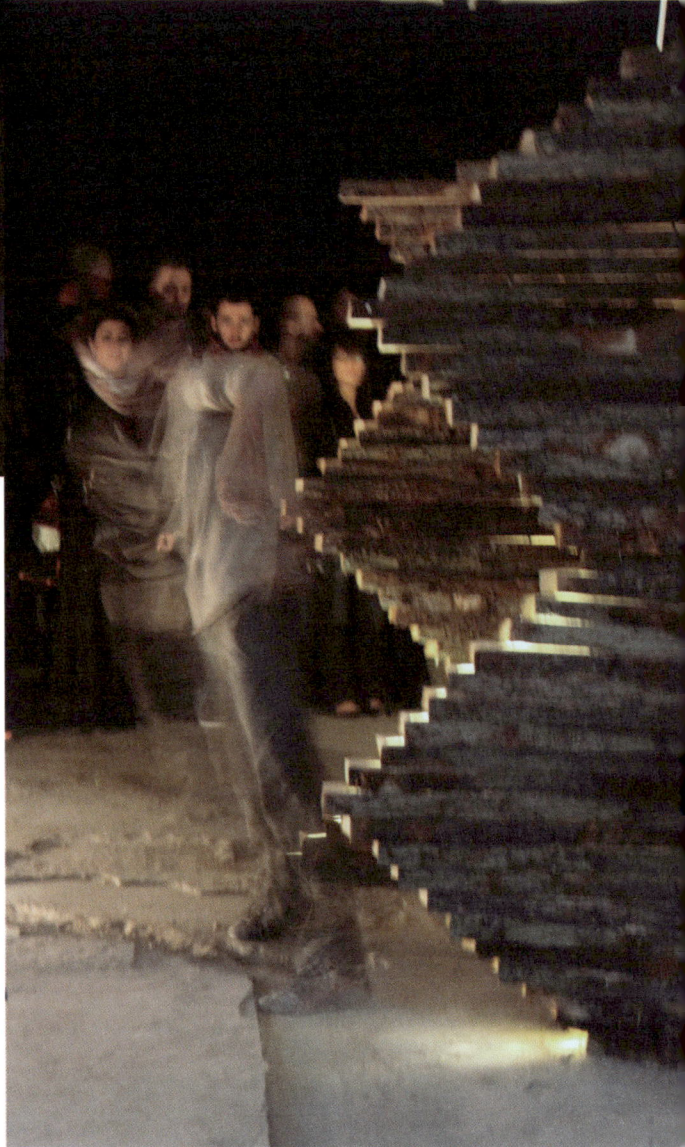

5.6
The "Hexadress" at the "Seed to
Scene/ S2S" festival in Covent
Garden in London 2010. (TH)

5.7
Renaud Wiser performing next
to the Timber Walls at the
Seed to Scene Festival. (TH)

5.8
Patricia Okenwa and Renaud Wiser "peeping" through the
walls at the audience during the New Movement Collective
Performance at the Seed to Scene festival.(TH)

5.9
Patricia Okenwa performing in the
"light room" underneath the hexagon
canopy at "Seed to Scene". (TH)

More generally, since even visual art was seen earlier to require the performative interaction of the beholder, this is even more obvious in architecture (Harman 2020). Architectural work without at least some peripheral function would be indistinguishable from sculpture. Indeed, this is precisely why Kant shows a certain disdain towards architecture since he sees its usefulness as spoiling the aesthetic 'purity' he demands from any work of art. And just as the later Fried acknowledged (against his own wishes) that artworks require the beholder's involvement, architectural form is inconceivable apart from someone's experience of it. This is already true of the viewer who gazes upon the stereotypical picture postcard view of a building's visual look but becomes even more so in the essentially kinetic and memory-driven experience of an edifice. This is true even of relatively passive contemplation of a building: hence we need not oppose 'events' to 'static' objects as Bernard Tschumi does, since even the apparently most frozen architectural stasis entails performative interaction between building and occupant (Khan, Hannah and Tschumi 2008).

The discourse of performance and objects, or objects 'in' performance, underlines the importance of the physical artefacts present within any given performance. Design and architecture, down to the smallest detail, form a central role in every performance and cannot be neglected, even or especially when the design aims to be absent or invisible. The awareness of this interrelated dependence of objects and performance makes 'performance design' a core testing and research ground for design considered broadly. Spatial performance teaches us about the objects of design, whether it be a question of architecture, products, or cities. Knowing how something (or better, some 'thing') is performing brings us to understand how it is connected with other elements and is therefore part of a larger framework. Designing an object entails the task of ensuring that this object can fully 'perform' within these networks with lasting effects, or even with unfolding potentials.

This becomes increasingly clear if one looks at individual objects of significance within a performance: as props that carry a large part of the burden in the overall production.

If you were to ask a random person to re-enact a theatrical performance, there is a substantial possibility that they would choose to mime Shakespeare's Hamlet with the skull of the deceased jester, "poor Yorik" (Shakespeare 2016). This prop, an object derived from a (deceased) subject, is the anchor of the entire performance, encapsulating the narrative, the dilemma, and indeed all human discourse in the play. Objects are always performing, regardless of whether they are part of a 'performance'. This gives them the power to create and underline narratives, and to embody symbolism and the history embedded within it. An object placed within a performance will instantly transport major parts of the narrative, the time, and even the political intent of the production. A performance of Hamlet would be drastically different if Yorik's skull were replaced with a 'natural' skull, a Mexican 'Calavera', or a Damien Hirst diamond-encrusted skull since the new references implied by each of these alternatives would themselves become part of the play. Even an imaginary skull, held in an empty hand, would leave the frame of reference entirely up to the spectator.

Bad Objects

One interesting variant of objects, especially in a performance context, is the 'bad object' There are several forms a bad object can take, with differing effects on the overall performance. One of these is the out-of-place object. In various forms of performance and media, most of us can recognise objects that are 'out of place' and which therefore spoil the overall artwork. One can recognise such carelessly placed objects as a plastic water bottle accidentally left in a period drama or photo shoot, thereby spoiling the entire illusion. But we can also recognise such unavoidable out-of-place objects as emergency exit signs or fire extinguishers found in sets and galleries. Again, and again such examples can be found. In parts of the documentation of many of our own projects, we have to carefully choose material that does not reveal objects that were left in the wrong place, often at the very moment of the performance itself: a drink forgotten next to the stage, the backpack with a vividly coloured change of clothing sticking out into the picture, or unused equipment left behind in plain sight. Such objects turn up especially in site-specific performances. For example, next to an industrial scissor lift that we used as a performance platform during our "Exquisite Corpse" performance in Cologne in 2011, the emergency and security signs were always prominently visible from almost all angles and stood out as 'out of place' in an otherwise entirely transformed space, even though they were the only objects actually 'belonging' to the place. In these cases, the objects drag the situation of the performance back into the framework of reality with its actual time and place, causing our minds to 'edit' the scene so as to purposely overlook these items.

Another form of 'bad objects' would be the poorly designed object. We speak here of objects that challenge the overall performance not primarily because of their outer appearance, but because their presence limits the possibilities of the overall performance. For example: costumes that prohibit dancers from moving or from interacting with each other, bodily extensions that cut into the performers' skin or simply cause them pain, or props and sets that present a safety risk for performers or audience, insofar as they were not designed to cope with the strenuous interactions unfolding within the performance.

A related category of objects, though not 'bad' in the strict sense, is that of fake or pretend objects. These range from painted sceneries to non-functional props. Such objects act as if they are another object. This could happen in the form of a 'realistic' representation, or in an abstract or exaggerated manner. To categorise fake or pretend objects as 'bad', we might have to assume that these objects are a poor representation of what they are envisioned to be. If a pretend object manages to become a 'sign' and is no longer seen as what it is, but as something else — as when a chair becomes a 'non-chair', as described by Freddie Rokem in "A Chair is a Chair is a CHAIR" (Rokem 1988) — then the transformation is successful. However, if these stand-in objects do not manage to become the other, due to a lack of a framework that supports this illusion through acting, lighting, or narrative, the objects are seen as the main culprit of bad design.

The same might be said about fake objects. If a 'non-functioning' object mimics an actual object, such as a paper table or bed, or a painted or projected landscape, its believability depends again on the surrounding framework. Waves in a mechanical theatre might be believable if they were set within a comical or pantomime environment; however, they would be entirely out of place if they were part of a stage performance based on Hemingway's "The Old Man and the Sea" (Hemingway 1995). The less believable an object is as a representation of others the more effort is required from all other elements of the performance to surpass these shortcomings. This becomes especially true in case of minimal or absent design or objects.

Minimal or Absent Design in Performance

One design mistake made by many creative people is the assumption that a thrown or rough or minimalist approach is easy. All too often, the opposite is true. Minimalist or 'sparse' sets and designs require extensive knowledge of the performance of objects. Some examples of this include imagined objects, black boxes, and fake or pretend objects.

An imagined object is formed in the mind of the performer and audience simultaneously, whether in the case of an actor holding up an invisible object, or a performer moving in an imagined space. Within the framework of performance, even in the absence of physical artefacts, these imagined objects require a high degree of design to be 'present' and relevant. These implied objects require some knowledge about them on the part of the creators, performers, and audience alike. The obligation to represent the absent object weighs heavily on the subjects surrounding it. The performer's movement and behaviour, the director's precision, and the understanding of the understanding must work all the harder to materialise the object.

The extension of the concept of the imagined object is that of the so-called 'black box', in a different sense from the usual cybernetic one (Latour 1987). What is meant here is the isolation of a single object against an empty black field, in which the blackness is the attempt to turn a space into a mind-space. All concentration is focused on the pure subject. We all know this from theatre and dance performances in which the performer is the only thing one sees, but also from a TV series such as "Stranger Things": at the moment when the lead character Eleven goes into her mind space, everything turns black except for the specific things that come into focus. In this way the blackness becomes the first framework of the performance as a whole, allowing us to focus on the things that must be seen, and thereby becoming the major object of design itself. Everything else must first contest the blackness and break through it. Spotlight, movement and even sound are dependent on it.

A counterpart to invisible objects in performance are the objects behind the scenes, the ones that should not be seen. Conversely, within performance these 'non-objects' are often the most important objects of all. They are the 'supporting' or 'enabling' objects, which are not supposed to be noticed. In order to function, they require an equally invisible yet highly skilled network of subjects behind the scenes. Here there is a wide range of objects to be considered, from 'gaffer tape' to other, more specialised technical equipment. Along with the usual fixed devices, many supporting objects can be developed 'ad hoc' in such a way as provide needed solutions or fixes: the pin in the poorly fitting costume, the aforementioned gaffer tape that holds up loose parts of the set, but also objects that distract or obscure views within the scene. In this way, these objects transform bad objects into functioning ones. Stated differently, they make these objects disappear precisely through their smooth functioning, as Martin Heidegger demonstrates in the famous tool-analysis of his masterwork "Being and Time" (Heidegger 2008, Harman 2002).

The Acting of Objects

Like actors, objects might have very different appearance and functionality according to whether they are on or off the stage. Whereas onstage they might need to be fixed and visible, whilst off-stage they might need to be packed up and whisked away instantly. For example, onstage objects need to disappear immediately during a change of scene and be stored out of sight. A primary visible object on stage, such as a building or landscape, needs to disappear into small boxes out of sight of the audience in the shortest possible time. The entire organisation of stagehands and roadies is designed around this need of transformation. The design for objects off-stage often requires as much consideration, if not more so, than the design of what is onstage. Logistics is the hidden half of any performance, and this is where the objects and people behind the scenes become the main protagonists. The performance starts to extend substantially beyond the time-frame of the visible. This becomes increasingly important in the case of travelling performances, which need to be adaptable to multiple different environments.

However, the capacity to transform and unfold is becoming more important as a part of performances themselves. With an increasing desire to create interactive and immersive performances, objects need to act, re-act, and change as part of the overall production. It is a central aim of performance to captivate the audience. In some sense the spectator should become one with the event, as described earlier in the case of the innate theatricality of painting and even of architecture, and as seen as far back as Artaud's "Theater of Cruelty" and the "Happenings" of 1960s art (Artaud 1994, Sontag 1966). Design, acting, performance, and direction aim to provide an effective bridge between the performance onstage and the mind of the observer. Theatrical effects help to build this illusion. Immersion in and interaction with the audience increasingly becomes a focus of the design of the objects and environment, especially given the powerful possibilities of today's technology. Real-time tracking of movement, as well as the reactiveness of props, lights, and sound to both actors and audience, create an 'active' role for objects in performances.

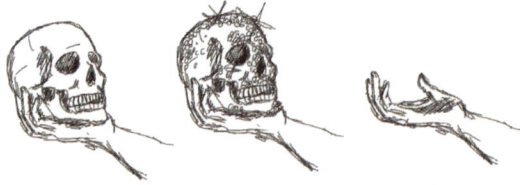

5.10
Sketch of three different
"skulls" of "hamlets" poor
Yorick. (TL)

5.11
New Movement Collective performing "Exquisite
Corpse" at the DQE in Cologne 2011 in an industrial
setting with "no smoking" and structures in sight. (VB)

5.12
Cloud and performer in black
box at the Matadero Madrid as
part of Flow Fields 2013. (SY)

5.13
Atimanyu Vashishth acting in a black box during the
performance "Parding your Beggon" as part of the "Moult"
festival at the Teatro Albert in Lisbon in 2023. (FA)

Performance allows us to re-appropriate objects, thereby extending their potential. The concept of the 'thrown' object becomes quite clear and visible within a staged environment: the table that becomes the stage or the prop, that 'stands in' for multiple other objects and subjects. Consider a piece of fabric that might serve by turns within the course of a single play as a curtain, a bundle in the form of a newborn child, and finally perhaps as a cloak. Such constant transformation allows us to re-evaluate the potentials of a given object. Because we are allowed to imagine, we might end up understanding a lot more about the object itself.

This re-evaluation of objects could be extended further by considering their design within the context of performance. Objects designed for performance do not have to follow the same rules as they would within other design or architectural settings, since the expressed aims for their performances differ in each case. They become 'exponential' objects. A structural concept that might aim at permanence and rigidity in a typical setting might need to give up these qualities temporarily, so as to allow for interaction with the performers or other objects, whilst still having to follow safety and security requirements. Such extended challenges might demonstrate, in turn, new possibilities that might feed back into overall design and engineering practice itself. The 'flimsy' design from the set becomes the initiator of new ideas far beyond its expressed function. These objects, designed for one context, might in this way develop many possibilities and initiate new ideas, projects, and performances in which their potential is explored further. They might become active beyond the stage and generate tangible after-effects.

Many of our design objects might follow this principle. The most prominent, however, would be the inflatable structure produced by the studio for the "Exquisite Corpse" series that took place in Cologne, Madrid, and London. From the start, a set of constraints influenced the design. The material we wanted to use were free off-cuts from the inflatable company "Inflate" in London. These pieces of rip-stop nylon were mostly narrow but lengthy leftovers of fabric that consequently produced numerous seams across any structure constructed from it. Nevertheless, we aimed at creating large-scale structures that could rapidly emerge within the scenery, representing foam bubbling up. The resulting design was a series of long, thin fabric tubes meeting at intersection points, with a multitude of seams and connections forming a Dodecahedron Tetrahedral Grid Structure. From a strictly engineering point of view, these premises would contradict the design practice of inflatable structures, where large pillows and a minimal number of seams are the basis of rigidity. However, the aim of the structures was not merely stability from the outset. The dancers were supposed to be able to interact with the structure, so as to make it perform and 'dance with and within them'. The structure was rigid enough to unfold and stand up by itself. However, the 'weak' points of the structure offered the opportunity for direct interaction: by suffocating separate elements of the grid, the overall structure started to breathe, and to interact with the performers. An extended definition of the 'performance' of the objects led to a new design approach challenging otherwise accepted rules. As a result, these structures became the most used and reused object of the studio, travelling to various events in Europe and the United States, unfolding and performing in a different environment and a different way each time. The object designed to 'perform with' became in fact the main performer.

Urban Performance and Objects

The extension of performance goes beyond the framed environment of sets or pre-established venues. Objects brought into existing environments might transform them in turn, making them part of the performance. These transformations might happen through bespoke adaptations or designs for specific locations. However, they might also happen through the mere presence of out-of-place objects that signify the takeover of the found realm.

In our context these out of place objects often are not overwhelming structures that in themselves represent a new construct or building, like the construction of a pavilion or small building would signify. The objects might be movable and relatable in scale to invite passers-by to interact with them. They truly come to life in the moment of performance, where the urban setting and objects, together with the subjects of performers and audience, form new relations and re-frame otherwise known situations.

This was the case during the performances of "The Walk" in Logroño in Spain in 2017 as part of the 4th Concéntrico Festival. Here triangulated wooden objects were placed on the main urban square. These objects were activated and recombined during the performance to form a multitude of geometries in reaction to dancers. The choreography of objects and subjects animated the audience to begin 'the walk' through the city with its various installations culminating in a performance within an old vine cellar with a full performance of the piece. The pieces of construction became the Pied Piper of Hamelin, luring the people into the performance.

Another example of objects in the urban realm would be that of "The Conversation" in 2014. As part of the "ReSet" festival in Barcelona the performance took over three different squares of the city. The performance was set around objects that represented sun, light, wind, inflation, and screen observed by a camera. Each of the elements was personified by a performer, bringing otherwise unnoticed and hidden elements into focus, as well as into constantly changing relations. On each urban square the performance, even though it was identical each time in terms of dramaturgy and choreography, transformed the site and its audience in a unique way.

5.14
The "Exponential Object" of the inflatable dodecahedron
structure of the Exquisite corpse series, spanning the
courtyard of the Architectural Association in 2011. (VB)

5.15
A set of inflatable dodecahedron structures as
a dynamic stage set for the "Exquisite Corpse"
events at the DQE in Cologne in 2011. (VB)

5.16
Triangular dynamic urban objects assembled through dance during the AAIS 2017 performance "A Walk" as part of Concetrico festival in Logroño. (TS)

5.17
New Movement Collective performing "The Conversation" as objects spectated by the "Camera" on Plaça Nova in Barcelona during the Reset festival in 2014. (HM)

Performance as Object of Protest and Politics

Within the discourse of performance and objects, a discussion about the political significance of objects within a performative environment should not be neglected. Objects in performance are placed under consideration and are therefore not neutral. The objects carry with them the symbolism they entail. The set tells us if the approach to a piece is conservative or progressive, even if the acting and the words are identical in two cases. Just consider that the outrage triggered by productions deemed to belong to a certain tradition, even whilst employing objects that seemingly belong to a different tradition, is omnipresent in the history of performance. The power of symbolism, reinterpretation and re-contextualisation of performances have often been a useful tool in this way for opposition within oppressive environments. Objects, unless specifically outlawed, have the potential to transport protest in a subliminal way, and are less prone to being pinpointed as suspect than are spoken or written words.

In turn, this raises the broader question of the role of objects in politics (Harman 2014). In general, modern political theory is polarised according to Left and Right orientations, both of them aligned according to a specific theory of human nature. For Left theorists such as Rousseau and Marx, the human is a naturally good or improvable creature subverted by a society gone awry (Rousseau 1992, Marx 1977). For the Right, as with Machiavelli or Schmitt, the human is a dangerous animal who dangerous nature does not fundamentally change across the millennia (Machiavelli 2008, Schmitt 2007). In their recent best-seller *The Dawn of Humanity*, David Graeber and David Wengrow challenge this alternative, but their alternative is simply to replace the 'good' or 'evil' human with an imaginative and experimental one (Graeber and Wengrow 2021). In this way, we are once again trapped in a conception of politics as revolving around human nature. But is it really possible to imagine the development of politics apart from consideration of such objects as coins, the steppe, hybrid corn, longboats, cannonballs, armoured vehicles, and Twitter? Here we are dealing with factors that mediate and redirect human political energies. The question has been raised by S.S. Strum and B. Latour in their joint article on baboons and opens the possibility of an even broader performative role for objects than the one addressed directly in this article (Strum and Latour 1987).

But whether we are talking about objects 'in' performance or 'of' performance, we can conclude that objects at all scales within a performative environment have the potential to carry significant agency far beyond the event itself. They can become important tools in a wider set of parameters, ranging from the personal realm all the way to the wider political sphere. As with all tools, we must be knowledgeable of how we use them and for what purpose. The design and use of objects therefore deserve our utmost attention and should neither be overlooked nor merely be used as the slavish accompaniment of trends or styles. These tools of performance are core elements of our culture, and thus have substantial reach and numerous implications. They are not just the accessories of human will: far from it, since the inherent properties of objects often shape that will more than they are commanded by human whim (Mitchell 2011).

References

Artaud, Antonin. *The Theater and its Double*, trans. M.C. Richards. New York: Grove Press, 1994.

Baudrillard, Jean. *Fatal Strategies*, trans. P. Beitchman & W.G.J. Niesluchowski. Los Angeles: Semiotext(e), 2008.

Baudrillard, Jean. *Seduction*, trans. B. Singer. London: Palgrave Macmillan, 1991.

Fried, Michael. *Absorption and Theatricality: Painting and Beholder in the Age of Diderot*. Chicago: University of Chicago Press, 1988.

Fried, Michael. *Courbet's Realism*. Chicago: University of Chicago Press, 1990.

Fried, Michael. *Manet's Modernism: or, The Face of Painting in the 1860s*. Chicago: University of Chicago Press, 1996.

Garcia, Tristan. "The Photographic Real," trans. S. Emanuel, *Glass Bead* 2016. https://www.glass-bead.org/article/the-photographic-real/?lang=enview

Graeber, David & David Wengrow. *The Dawn of Everything: A New History of Humanity*. New York: Farrar, Straus and Giroux, 2021.

Harman, Graham. *Architecture and Objects*. Minneapolis: University of Minnesota Press, 2022.

Harman, Graham. *Art and Objects*. Cambridge: Polity, 2020.

Harman, Graham. *Bruno Latour: Reassembling the Political*. London: Pluto, 2014.

Harman, Graham. *Tool-Being: Heidegger and the Metaphysics of Objects*. Chicago: Open Court, 2002.

Heidegger, Martin. *Being and Time*, trans. J. Macquarrie & E. Robinson. New York: Harper, 2008.

Hemingway, Ernest. *The Old Man and the Sea*. New York: Scribner, 1995.

Kant, Immanuel. *Critique of Judgment*, trans. W. Pluhar. Indianapolis: Hackett, 1987.

Khan, Omar, Dorita Hannah, & Bernard Tschumi. "Performance/Architecture: An Interview with Bernard Tschumi," *Journal of Architetural Education* 61.4 (May 2008), pp. 52–58.

Latour, Bruno. *Science in Action: How to Follow Scientists and Engineers Through Society*. Cambridge: Harvard University Press, 1987.

Machiavelli, Niccolò. *The Prince*, trans. P. Bondanella. Oxford: Oxford University Press, 2008.

Marx, Karl. *Das Kapital*, Vol. 1, trans. B. Fowkes. New York: Vintage, 1977.

Mitchel, Timothy. *Carbon Democracy: Political Power in the Age of Oil*. London: Verso, 2011.

Rokem, Freddie. "A chair is a Chair is a CHAIR: The Object as Sign in the Theatrical Performance," in *The Prague School and Its Legacy*, pp. 275–288, ed. U. Tobin, Amsterdam: John Benjamins Publishing Company, 1988

Rose, Barbara. *American Art Since 1900*. New York: Praeger, 1975.

Rousseau, Jean-Jacques. *Discourse on the Origin of Inequality*, trans. D. Cress. Indianapolis: Hackett, 1992.

Sayre, Henry M. "The Object of Performance: Aesthetics in the Secenties," *The Georgia Review* 37.1 (Spring 1983), pp. 169–188.

Schmitt, Carl. *The Concept of the Political*, trans. G. Schwab. Chicago: University of Chicago Press, 2007.

Shakespeare, William. *Hamlet*. Revised Edition, London: Bloomsbury, 2016.

Sontag, Susan. "Happenings: An Art of Radical Juxtaposition," in *Against Interpretation: And Other Essays*, pp. 263–274. New York: Picador, 1966.

Strum, Shirley & Latour, Bruno. "Redefining the Social Link: From Baboons to Humans," *Social Science Information* 26.4 (1987), pp. 783–802.

6

Theo Lorenz
Tanja Siems

BEHIND THE SCENES

This glossary of anecdotes aims to provide comprehensive information on all facets of the development phase involved in creating applied projects. The focus of this chapter is on the origins of various performances, which are conceived and cultivated within a collaborative and interdisciplinary work environment. Following each show, during our question-and-answer sessions, the audience is inquiring about the particulars of developing these applied projects within the structure of practical teaching and learning conditions within a theoretical academic institution. When it comes to spatial performance and design, the focus of what we see is the performances themselves. We see everything 'at work' and working in a moment. It is temporal and unique, unfolding in the moment itself. The documentation of these moments might capture some highlights in images and video; however, it is virtually impossible to transport the whole show. It becomes even more difficult if we want in addition to reveal the methodologies, theoretical approaches, and processes behind the scenes. After each show, these exchanges often lead to more detailed inquiries about how such applied projects are developed within the complex construct of practical teaching and learning conditions inside a theoretical academic institution.

The projects are invented and created within the AAIS framework of pedagogic methodologies, based on an open design process within various cultural and social experiences and shared ownership in the collective. The AAIS participants acknowledge that design needs to evolve within a network of creative actors, sustainable materials and adaptable tools, in order to achieve a holistic approach for the final production phase. We show how it is possible to make these enormous projects happen within an ensemble of various disciplines and cultural backgrounds, through academic frameworks grounded in diverse applied pedagogies, despite financial restrictions and limiting legal regulations.

To produce a performative project the collective of creators need in addition to materials and performers as a basic requirement movement, space, sound, and projection. Hence, choreography needs a skilled composition of movement and dance; the space integrates architectural constructions and needs in its design process with creative, organisational, and productive skills. The element of sound needs the arrangement of music by a live orchestra or is created as a music production through technology; the projection fields and light installations can create an interactive environment to show the dramaturgy through film or spoken words and through highlighting the different elements within the performance.

Areas of Research

The Interprofessional Studio has spent years researching various areas that serve as the foundation for their overall approach and methodologies. Frameworks developed through sequences of projects that span over four years, with each project building upon the previous one.

The first area of research, which was completed from 2008 to 2012, focused on the impact of networks on collaboration and creative practice. The studio aimed to investigate the influence of teamwork within the creative field, specifically focusing on the question of how different actants invent and work together and what they create in actor networks. We examined how these collaborations can shape the design and creation of the performance itself. By creating relationships between actants and design, and encouraging collaboration across different disciplines, the studio was able to develop innovative approaches to designing performative spaces and objects that formed the basis of the approach of our studio. The four projects undertaken during this phase of research were "Bauhaus Lab" (2008), "Seed to Scene" (2009), "Exquisite Corpse" (2010), and "Angles of Incidence" (2011).

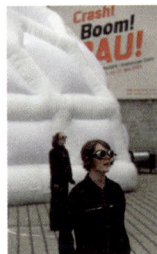

From 2012 to 2016 in the second area of research the AAIS explored the influence of collaborative networks on spatial dimensions, design, and objects. This research phase aimed to understand how networks impact various dimensions beyond creative practice. As the research progressed, the focus shifted to the interplay among physical space, external environments, artistic design and tangible elements in performance. The studio explored how collaborative networks influence the way we design spaces, objects, and other elements of performance. We investigated how the use of networks can change the way we perceive and interact with space, how it can shape our understanding of objects, and how it can influence the design of the physical environment. The studio completed four projects during this period, namely Open source: "Flow Fields" (2012), "The Conversation" (2013), "Moving Stone" (2014) and "UnREAL: XYZ's" (2015).

The third research phase took place from 2016 to 2020 and was centred on the political implementation of performance as a form of protest. This phase of research aimed to examine the interplay between design and culture and the social and political environment. Cultural practices and beliefs are shaped by the social and political environment in which they exist, and how it is shaped by design and culture. Music, fashion, and art of a particular ethos reflects the beliefs and values of the society that created them. Equally cultural artefacts have an impact on the society, reinforcing or challenging existing beliefs and values. The studio completed four projects during this period, namely "Trust, Truth, Integrity" (2016), "A Walk" (2017), "Others: Portrait of Human" (2018) and "Scream out loud!" (2019).

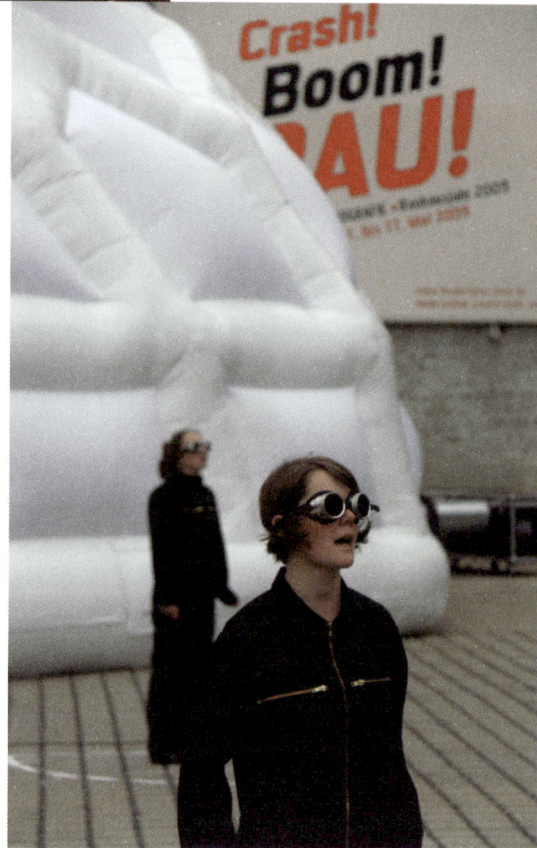

6.1
Rehearsal for "Moult" in Lisbon
at the Teatro Aberto with AAIS
students and staff in 2023. (TS)

6.2
Performance of the young theatre group Infront of AAIS's
inflatable structure as part of the "Bauhaus Lab" and the
"crash boom bau" scenography festival in Jena 2009.(TH)

6.3
Performance "A Walk" as part of Concéntrico
festival in Logroño with Dancers from the Trinity
Laban Conservatoire of Music and Dance. (TS)

6.4
New Movement Collective
performing "Moving Stone" at
Pikes on Ibiza in 2015. (DK)

The latest research phase, which started in 2020 and ran until 2023, focuses on the question of identity and responsibility, particularly as creatives. As creatives we have a unique perspective and ability to influence and shape the world around us through our work. However, this also means that there is a certain level of responsibility that comes with that influence, as we explore further in the chapter Compassion. In the context of the Interprofessional Studio, this research phase investigated how identity intersects with creative practice. This included questions such as: How do individuals and groups define and express their identities through their creative work? How does identity influence the creative process and the resulting work? What responsibility do creatives have in representing and advocating for different identities in their work? How can creatives use their work to address social and political issues related to identity and representation? By examining these questions and considering the role of identity and responsibility in the creative practice we develop new insights and approaches to creating work that is more inclusive, ethical, and resonant. The studio explores the complex relationship between identity and responsibility within the creative field through four projects: "Origin" (2020), "Wherefore Art Tough" (2021), "Echo" (2022), and "Moult" (2023).

Since 2024, the studio has entered a new research phase titled "Compassionate Change". This phase builds on the preceding inquiries into identity by asking how care, empathy, and responsibility can be translated into structural and systemic transformation. The first brief, "The Estranged Gaze of Compassion" (2024), explored Brechtian distancing and intellectual empathy in performance. The 2025 brief, "The Fable of Our Children", drew on the writings of James Baldwin to examine freedom, protest, and intergenerational imagination. The next brief in the series is "The Principle of Hope" (2026), which takes inspiration from Ernst Bloch's philosophy to investigate performative strategies that imagine the not-yet — forms of resistance and collaboration that point beyond the present toward possible futures.

Translating these philosophical commitments into practice, the studio addresses how performative and spatial strategies can embody compassionate change. This includes practices such as using environmentally conscious materials in set and costume design, reducing energy consumption during rehearsals and performances, and implementing inclusive casting and collaboration models. Beyond environmental concerns, the phase engages with systemic questions: how can performance and design reflect structures of care, equity, and shared responsibility? What does it mean to build frameworks that support not only sustainability, but also participation and long-term cultural resilience? A compassionate culture in theatre and spatial practice responds to crisis not with retreat, but through solidarity, transformation, and imaginative resistance. The research phase "Compassionate Change", running from 2024 to 2027, continues to unfold through four performative projects developed in collaboration with international partners and institutions across Europe.

People

Across the various articles in this book, we mention case studies and people. Many of them are part of the AAIS core team for years now. Each with their unique yet overlapping signature with each representing a unique area of responsibility. We have an incredibly talented and diverse team of individuals who are all experts in their respective fields, and we're absolutely thrilled to be collaborating on all the projects together. Each member of our team brings a unique area of expertise, but our specialties also overlap, allowing us to work collaboratively and create something truly remarkable.

We've got Argyris Angeli, a fantastic artist and performance specialist with a strong background in architecture. Mona Camille brings her skills as a stage designer and architect, with a focus on artistic delivery. Nerma Cridge is an architect and educator specialising in academic writing. Andy Dean is a sound artist and producer with long-standing ties to the studio. Malgorzata Dzierzon is a choreographer and producer with wide experience in collaborative work. Heiko Kalmbach is a dramaturg, filmmaker, and advocate. Theo Lorenz is our director and for decades an artist, media designer, architect, and educator. David McAlmont contributes as a performer, singer-songwriter, and art historian. Patricia Okenwa is a choreographer and producer. Mauricio Pauly is a composer involved in several of our sound-based works. Thomas Parkes is a musician and AV specialist. Pierre Nedd contributes as a music producer and DJ. Joel Newman is a video artist and AV designer. Kyriaki Nasioula is a producer with expertise in choreography and architecture. Gemma Nixon is a choreographer and movement instructor. Noa Segev manages venue relations and is also an architect. Hila Shemer is a writer, journalist, and architect. Tanja Siems, as co-founder, focuses on research and participation in urban design. Atimanyu Vashishth is a performance maker and poet working through a framework called 'Devised Domesticities'. Renaud Wiser is our studio manager, mover, and choreographer. Yoav Ronel is a writer and theorist focusing on poetic representations of love, idleness, and critique. All are actively involved as part of the core studio team and continue to contribute to the ongoing development of its work.

Each of these team members has an extensive field of knowledge that helps to constantly grow our field of innovation and work. As this is the first / (slash) in the series of /people books, it needs to be continued with a series of publications to represent the different exponential pathways of the team of alumni, as all the case studies and areas of new work and research emerging from the studio, need a lot more space to unfold.

How we meet

Every year the Interprofessional Studio is working with a set of new and interesting collaborators. This way we meet and start to collaborate is often different and surprising. Whereas the studio organises the bigger framework for each set up of the years, new collaborations and connections happen in different scales and size. They are emerging from different members of the team, be it a member of the teaching staff, a student, an alumnus or an institutional partner.

Although most of our collaborations began in an unusual and interesting way, a few stories stand out. During the preparations for one of our first event "Seed 2 Scene", one of our students, Eugen Soler, approached us and mentioned that he is friends with a young choreographer and dancer, and if it would be interesting for the festival, if we could add a dance performance. At the time we had worked with musicians, scenographers, film producer and interactive designers but not yet with dancers. In the first instant we were quite sceptical, as we associated with dance and architecture more approaches that show performances 'in' architecture, added as entertainment for a museum opening, rather than a dialogue between space and movement.

However, when for the first meeting Eugen's friend Patricia Okenwa appeared together with Jonathan Goddard, Joe Walkling, Gemma Nixon and Renaud Wiser, a discussion emerged instantly about new forms of collaboration, flat hierarchies of networks and spatial explorations. As we showed a shared interest in these areas of work, we decided to collaborate on a performance in our Venue in Covent Garden. As we asked them how we should announce them, the group quickly decided that they would call themselves the "New Movement Collective", a group of choreographers and dancers we still collaborate with today.

In a more recent occurrence, we visited our friend and colleague Paula Cadima in Lisbon. One of the evenings she was meeting her cousin and husband in a nearby restaurant. We only briefly passed by the restaurant to say hello and Paula introduced us to Vera Sao Payo and João Lourenço, who kindly invited us to see a show at their Teatro Aberto the next day. When we arrived at the theatre Vera welcomed us, introduced us to the play that was on and, to our surprise, presented us with a series of detailed questions about the Interprofessional Studio and opened an intriguing discussion about its possible relations and differences to narrative-based theatre, performance and education and the environment. Based on this discussion Vera and João invited us to stage a performance at their theatre the following year, allowing us to test new forms of performance in narrative spaces.

Like-minded groups and individuals are everywhere. Besides direct approaches, recommendations through friends, extended professional partners and institutional links, new and lasting collaborations and connections occur in every situation. We should be open-minded and generous, but as well curious and flexible to find opportunities to collaborate. We recognise a genuine interest if equal excitement and curiosity is present on all sides. We should not instantly thing only of our 'repercussions', and if the others 'want' anything from us, or vice versa, but more of how one another can enrich and positively challenge each other's way of working.

Helping hands and mind

One of the most fulfilling elements of our work of the Interprofessional Studio is how we always extend constantly our network of collaboration. Each locality and each project brings with it a huge amount of collaboration, exchange of ideas and hands-on experience. This begins at home, where the extended AA team across all departments supports the work of the AAIS programme and its processes, adding specific knowledge and expertise. At the studio itself, but occasionally as well on-site craftsmanship from the AA maintenance team Colin Prendergast, Leslaw Skrzypiec and Mariusz Stawiarski helping us to build and change the immediate studio and settings for the various events.

Occasionally, in our fast-paced learning environment, which involves live events and a large team of students, who may have little to no prior experience in Audio-Visual (AV) production, mistakes are made. It is never our intention to break anything, but it can happen due to the steep learning curve. In such situations, we are fortunate to have an exceptional Audio-Visual department that has consistently shown immense patience, dedication and professionalism. Over the years, we have worked with outstanding individuals like Joel, Sepehr, Tom, Ben and Bert, who have gone above and beyond to ensure that our events run smoothly despite any challenges that arise. Their expertise and willingness to guide us through any difficulties are invaluable, and we are grateful for their continuous support. We have met similar dedication and help at every venue we have worked at: From the Matadero in Madrid to the Concéntrico Festival in Logroño, to the Teatro Aberto in Lisbon and the LabTec facilities in London. For our remote location in Seoul, Beijing and Shanghai, we always did find a reliable network of collaborators that made the process more professional, inclusive and exciting.

The mundane, anecdotal and serendipitous

Whereas we try to discuss the methodological and theoretical approach from different angles within this book, we want to reveal as well on the one hand the mundane processes of a creative project, as well as the anecdotal and serendipitous moments along the way. In any creative project, there are moments that seem mundane or routine, yet they are essential to the process. These are the daily tasks that keep the project moving forward, such as checking emails, making phone calls, and scheduling meetings. Although they may seem small and unremarkable, they are the background that make up the bigger picture.

However, there are also moments of serendipity that occur during the creative process, which can often lead to unexpected and exciting results. These moments of serendipity can occur in a variety of ways, such as stumbling upon a new idea whilst having a coffee with a peer at the AA bar or discovering a new technique whilst experimenting with materials in the workshop.

6.5
"Metamorph" performance as part
of the 2023 "Moult" festival at
the Teatro Aberto in Lisbon. (AR)

6.6
Musicians working together and rehearsing
with Andy Dean for the "Exquisite Corpse"
performance at the Matadero Madrid 2011. (HW)

6.7
"Seed to Scene"
structure discussion
and testing. (TS)

6.8
Renaud Wiser working with the performers
form "the place" during the "Moult" festival at
the Teatro Aberto in Lisbon. (TS)

6.9
Origin festival project Cybersapiens
in Shanghai build-up and rehearsal
discussion of the event via zoom. (TS)

Through the years there have been anecdotal moments that play a significant role in our creative process. These are the stories of personal experiences that inspire and inform the work. These anecdotes can add depth and richness to the work, providing a unique perspective that may not have been considered otherwise. These moments behind the scenes all contribute to the creative process in their own way. Whilst the theoretical and methodological approach is important, it's these moments that can often make the biggest impact on the final product. By embracing these moments and allowing them to guide the work we as artists and creators can discover new and exciting avenues that may have otherwise gone undiscovered.

How we Concentrate
Taking care of one another and initiating creativity amidst a complex network of ideas and influences is a fundamental aspect of our work. Providing emotional support is essential for the success of our projects, and it is an area of engagement that is continually growing within the realm of education for all tutors. As teachers and mentors, we recognise the importance of not only imparting knowledge but also being confidants and advisers to our students and team members. This extends to our team's various specialisations, such as Heiko Kalmbach, who, as a dramaturg, possesses extensive knowledge in advocacy from his work with various initiatives. Additionally, we focus on the overall well-being of our team, including movement, through Patricia Okenwa's series of movement sessions that are tailored to support our students' physical and mental health.

In this way, we recognise that creativity and productivity are deeply connected to our emotional and physical well-being. By providing support for our team members and students, we create an environment that nurtures creativity and encourages innovation. We understand that each individual is unique, and their needs may differ. Therefore, we strive to provide tailored support that meets the specific needs of each team member and student. Our approach to emotional support and well-being is an integral part of our creative process, and we believe that it is key to our success as a team.

iPhone Tower
Although we strive for a flat organisational structure in our work, there are occasions where a top-down approach seems necessary. One such example is the 'iPhone tower' that we use during our sessions. We are all highly addicted to our mobile devices. For research, communication, news and entertainment, these objects dominate every space. The practice of switching off mobile phones in theatres is a common practice that is widely observed in performing arts venues. The main reason for this is to minimise distractions during the performance, both for the performers and for the audience.

Theatrical performances require a high degree of concentration and focus from both the actors and the audience. Any external noise or light can be extremely distracting and disrupt the performance. A ringing phone, a text message alert or a flashlight can break the spell of the performance and spoil the experience for everyone. Switching off phones also shows respect for the performers and their work. It demonstrates a willingness to fully engage with the performance and allowing the audience to fully engage with the story being told.

We believe the same is true for a learning environment and thus we sometimes see the need to implement this practice as well during our studio sessions. To address this issue, we ask everyone to place their phones in a tower in the centre of the room, so that they can concentrate on the tasks at hand without any distractions. This practice has proven to be effective in the past, but it's not without its challenges. The temptation to check one's phone can be overwhelming, and we've observed that even the most disciplined of individuals struggle to resist the urge.

Out of your comfort zone

At times, where we have a constant evolving discourse in regard to identity, gender, and ethnicity, it becomes an imperative to not look at these issues in isolation, but rather look at how hierarchical, dominating and separating structures that enable inequality can be overcome altogether through new frameworks that enable us to thrive together. Every year our academic agenda within an international network is addressing the topics of protest, performance, and identity in a global challenging political environment. All participants in the programme are taking responsibilities as individuals in the right moment. Everyone, educator and student, needs to get out of their own comfort zone and have to integrate themselves during the whole creation and production phase. Here are some samples:

In one academic year a fashion designer was put to the task to develop the structural architectural and engineering plans for the inflatable extension building created by the Studio for the Theatre in Jena during the Bauhaus anniversary celebration. She was trained to design and produce wearable products, hence the challenge for her was to scale up everything she knows in order to plan and build with the whole team a fabric-based structure. The knowledge from her, how to handle different materials was of most importance for the entire team. When the inflatable structure was built, the student created an inflatable dress, which was acting as a mediator between the new build structure as the extension of the Theatre and the urban environment with its public square and inhabitants. This dress was then used as the icon for the advertisement of the scenography festival in Jena. The learning curve through this experience was immense, as she used her fashion design background to transform it into a build structure and with this new knowledge, she transferred it back into fashion.

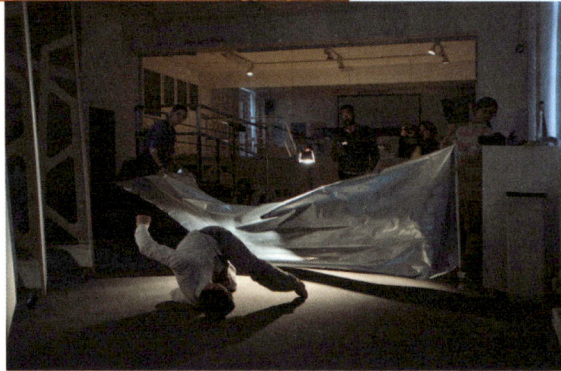

6.10
Structural experiments at Hooke
Park Workshop tor "Trust,
Truth Integrity project. (TS)

6.11
Experimental rehearsals
in the Studio with New
Movement Collective. (TL)

6.12
Projection of the inflatable dress on
the AAIS inflatable theatre during the
"Crash Boom Bau" festival in Jena. (TH)

6.13
Laura Boffi in her inflatable dress, as the
interactive 'agent', representing the bigger
construction of the inflatable theatre. (TH)

In parallel to the design phase of the inflatable structure an artist, who was working during his former practice completely by himself and never in a collective, got the task to organise the whole building team. This was for him a great networking exercise to generate these complex schedules during the production phase. Therefore, as a trained individual artist, he had to always have the complete overview of the workload and the production process within the team. These are only two samples from our interprofessional work process over the last fifteen years.

To work out of your comfort zone could be challenging but it is essential for all of us to learn and create within other disciplines. We are trusting each individual member in our AAIS network, and each year the collectively created applied projects are always beyond our expectations.

Moments of creation and success

The moments when everything falls into place and aligns perfectly are the moments making all the hard work and effort worthwhile. Often, these moments are just a split second away from chaos and disorder. It could be the first successful performance of a play, just minutes after a disastrous dress rehearsal. It could be the moment when the audience reacts with laughter at the perfect moment in a thought-provoking piece.

It's also the moment when you take a break from your own work and appreciate the creativity and professionalism of your colleagues. Furthermore, it's the moments of harmony when the entire team is relaxing during a mindfulness exercise, or when multiple things are happening simultaneously but in perfect synchronicity during a design session or rehearsal.

We encounter many of these situations in our creative work and it's important to take a moment to pause and appreciate them. Doing so can be vital for our mental well-being during intense and exciting processes of creation. Recognising these moments can help us stay motivated and energised to continue pushing through the challenges and obstacles that arise during the creative process.

How we Celebrate

We have the unique opportunity to work on events and festivals, which not only provide us with the chance to showcase our creative work but also give us a reason to celebrate. Despite the high stress and pressure that comes with organising events, we always manage to come together as a team and create work beyond our expectation. The festivals we produce are not only a platform for staging our designs but also a space for artists, performers and musicians to showcase their talents.

One of the best things about these festivals is that the celebration doesn't stop after the show ends. We keep the party going with music events and celebrations that feature some of the best musicians and DJs in the industry. Our team includes acclaimed music producer and DJ Andy Dean, as well as the talented singer and songwriter David McAlmont, to curate a diverse line up of music events that range from dance music and jazz to experimental and avant-garde sounds. We also collaborate with Mauricio Pauly's "Distractfold Ensemble," a contemporary music ensemble that specialises in experimental music, to ensure that our music events offer a wide spectrum of genres and styles. Our celebrations are always inspiring, and the party only ends when we're forced to shut down. The festivals we produce are not just events but unforgettable experiences that leave a lasting impression on our audiences, but as well ourselves.

Creative participatory Places

Spaces for performance, collaboration and creation can refer to physical or virtual spaces where we as artists, performers and creators come together to collaborate and showcase our work. These places can vary in size, location, and type of venue and they can be both local and international. Local places as London-based spaces and sites for performance, collaboration, and creation can be beside our own AAIS studio at the Architectural Association; other places like empty buildings, as we used for the "Seed to Scene" project in Covent Garden or for "Portrait of Human" at Nest, a space in Soho. For the festival "Origins" in Camden or the "Echo" festival at Heals, we used art galleries or previous retail units to showcase the projects of our students. In addition, theatres and concert halls are good places for our festivals including the performances, such as the Watermans Art Centre in London which we could use for XYZ's Project. These types of venues are often more accessible to local artists and audiences, and they provide opportunities for our emerging artists to show their work.

Collaborative and innovative performances can be created in international settings that encompass renowned theatres like the Teatro Aberto in Lisbon, cultural institutions such as the Matadero Madrid or the Xue Museum in Beijing, where we have successfully organised festivals together. We also participate in established festivals like the performance festival in Jena as part of the "Bauhaus Lab", and the Concéntrico Festival in Logroño, where our AAIS project "A Walk" was showcased. Furthermore, we engage with biennial and triennial events such as the Krakow Biennale or the Lisbon Triennale, where the "Flow Field" project participated in the opening event of the year-long celebration. These international venues offer valuable networking opportunities, collaboration prospects, and wider exposure to diverse cultures, perspectives, and artistic practices. Additionally, we explore urban and unconventional spaces that complement the internal venues, creating vibrant areas for performances and engaging interactions with the audience. An example of this was the ReSet Festival in Barcelona, where our project "The Conversation" took place.

6.14
Build-up of the inflatable structure
with the team of Inflate and the
Theaterhaus Jena for the "Crash
Boom Bau" festival 2009. (PA)

6.15
Projection of projects on the
AAIS inflatable theatre during
the "Crash Boom Bau" festival
in Jena. (TH)

6.16
The twenty by twenty
by ten-meter Inflatable
structure before build-up
in two bags. (TH)

6.17/18/19/20
Moments of creation and success during the
production for the flow field festival at the
Roca Gallery in London in 2013. (TS/TL/SY)

6.21
Rehearsing at the DQU for Exquisite Corpse
with the Music Ensemble from Cologne and
New Movement Collective. (VB)

6.22
Participation of Performers from Cologne, Madrid and London
in AAIS Project "Angles of incident" creating a collaborative
performance between professionals and local participants. (VB)

6.23
Audience participation during
the events of "Angles of Incident"
at the Matadero Madrid. (VB)

Nowadays, we need to consider the virtual realm as well; as we all experienced very directly during the 2020 pandemic. Virtual spaces which are accommodating performances are becoming increasingly an extension to the physical events and can include online platforms for live streaming performances, virtual reality environments for immersive experiences, and digital collaboration tools for remote collaboration. As places we need to consider all the unseen places as well, that are literally behind the scenes, as we spend most of our time in these spaces. Workshops, studio spaces and cafés; but as well, rehearsal spaces, computer labs and green rooms are the backbone of all work.

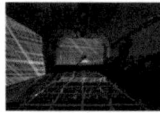

Elements as Light and Projections

Lighting and projections are pivotal components of our performance design, serving to set the tone, build atmosphere, and convey messages. Using specialised lighting and projection equipment, we can manipulate the space and create an immersive environment that transports the audience to new realms. By artfully balancing light intensity we can emphasise significant moments, convey a sense of emotion and add depth to the performance.

Furthermore, by overlaying visual projections onto the stage, designers can create effects, augmenting the live-action and enabling the audience to experience the events in an extended way. From the subtlety of dimmed lighting to the grandeur of elaborate projection mapping and virtual realities, lighting and projections are essential to the creation of a dynamic, engaging, and truly memorable performance. The challenge here is precision and timing that requires the students to master as part of their artistic work. They not only have to be able to set and use the lights in environments we fully control but need to be, in addition, able to communicate these tasks with professionals at the different venues.

Senses and Haptic habitat

As designers and performers, we understand that the spaces we create are not just physical structures, but also environments that engage all of the senses. We believe that the audience should be fully immersed in the experience, using all their senses to understand and interact with the environment in unique ways.

To achieve this, we employ a variety of methods to engage the senses during our performances. For example, during a festival in Madrid, we designed installations and performances in a spacious, dark space. The audience was seated comfortably in cocoon-like hammocks and could feel the live performing musicians moving around the entire area during the concert. After the sound performance, light revealed the spatial design elements that were created specifically for the space.

The audience was invited to explore the space, touch the unique materials used for the installations, and smell the different scents. This haptic experience was followed by a culinary food experience where visitors could observe the preparation of fresh vegetables cooked by local vendors. The final presentation and discussion of the artistic project with creators, experts, and visitors were further enlightened by this sensory experience. Through these different approaches, we aimed to make the audience experience the cultural setting of the venue in a unique and memorable way.

In Cologne, we placed the emphasis on the sense of taste as the main element of our performance. Live musicians were placed throughout the space, and dancers moved around a food-stand structure erected in the centre of the room. Visitors were invited to walk to the food-stand and experience a culinary delight whilst being in motion and watching the performance. This approach allowed the audience to animate the dancers and influence the performance by moving around and interacting with them.

We believe that engaging all the senses in our performances creates a deeper, and more immersive experience for the audience. Our goal is to provide a multi-sensory and haptic habitat that allows the audience to interact with the space and the performers in a unique, and unforgettable way.

Audience participation

In spatial performance and design, the role of the audience is expanded beyond that of traditional theatre. The spatial division between the audience and the performance is intertwined, with the audience being actively encouraged to participate and interact with the actors, objects, and themes throughout the performance. This results in unique and unpredictable experiences that are capable of surprising and delighting the audience.

However, achieving the optimal balance between audience participation and personal space can be a challenging task. Some audience members may be hesitant to engage, whilst others may become excessively enthusiastic and disrupt the performance. We, as designers and organisers, must therefore manage this delicate balance, ensuring that personal boundaries are not violated whilst still facilitating immersive and engaging interaction. The success of interaction within our spatial performance and design depends on the audience's willingness and ability to actively participate. Managing this relationship is essential to creating an immersive and unforgettable experience.

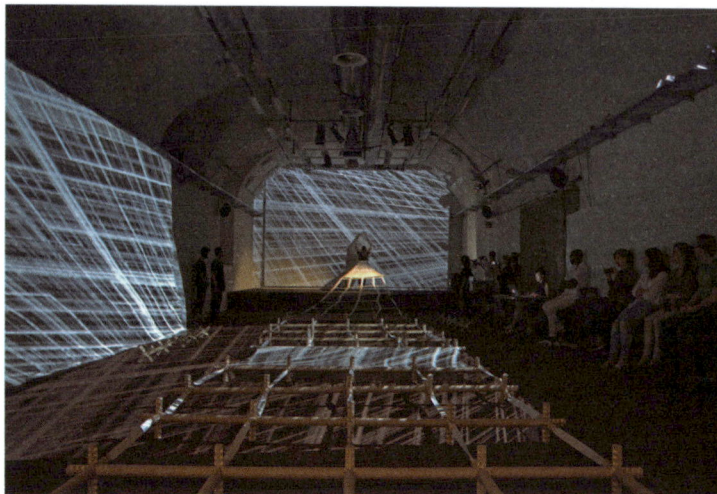

6.24
Audience integration during the events through light and projections in "Superposition" as part of the "XYZ" series at the Architecture Center of the MuseumsQuartier, in Vienna 2016. (VB)

6.25
Sound experience with musicians from London and the "Musikhochschule" in Cologne at the Matadero Madrid as part of "Angles of incident" events Madrid. (VB)

6.26
Sound and food experience during "Angles of Incident" at Cultural Centre in Cologne. (TS)

6.27
Collaborative participation and
interaction with architecture during
a workshop at Conservatoire of
Music and Dance. (TL)

Notations as a communicator

In interdisciplinary environments, graphical explanations and notations are needed to aid in communication between experts from different fields. However, some systems based on symbols can be out of sync, and there is a need for notations that are immediately visual. In architecture, notations are also important. Bernard Tschumi explores the relationship between architecture and event in the urban context, and he includes diagrams and notations to represent his ideas (Tschumi 2005). He uses dynamic notational systems, such as his use of arrows and lines to indicate movement and flow within a space. His approach to notation emphasises the importance of visual communication in the design process and the need for architects to think about space in terms of its experiential qualities.

To produce notations within creative disciplines as a communicator for the entire process is used by artists across different disciplines. For example, the artists John Cage, Takehisa Kosugi and James Tenney collaborated on a series of works known as "Musicircus" in the 1960s, in which multiple musical events would occur simultaneously in a given space. Cage developed a graphic notation system to allow for the coordination of these events, which he called "Time–Bracket Notation" (Cage 1969). This system consisted of horizontal lines representing time and vertical brackets indicating when a sound should begin and end. The composer Roland Kayn is another example of an artist who made use of graphic notation in his work (Patterson 1968). Kayn developed a complex system of symbols and diagrams to represent different sonic elements, allowing for the creation of highly detailed and intricate compositions. As well as the musician Douglas Leedy, he uses notations as a way of creating and communicating his various compositions as shown in his piece "Entropical Paradise". In this work, he used a combination of traditional musical notation and graphic symbols to represent both musical and non-musical elements, such as breathing and movement.

In the field of dance, the choreographer Merce Cunningham also made use of graphic notation in his work (Cunningham 1968). Cunningham collaborated with several composers throughout his career, including John Cage, who often created the music for his dances (Miller 2001, p. 545-552). Cunningham's notation system consisted of a series of symbols representing different movements and gestures. Similarly, Rudolf Laban, a pioneer of modern dance, developed a system of dance notation known as "Labanotation" (Guest 1974). This system uses symbols and diagrams to represent movements and gestures, allowing for the precise notation of a dance performance.

This tradition translates into the practice of the course where notation becomes a necessary means to bridge different ways of communicating between disciplines and languages as well as space. A good example is a notation made by Young Eun Kim, who used as part of the AAIS 2013 Flow Fields the Korean characters and their relation to mouth movements to provide notations for the musicians of the "Distractfold Ensemble". The ensemble itself is used to working with graphical notations as Mauricio Pauly composes the various complex sound pieces in spatial, colourful graphical representations, that can fully represent the multiple dimensions and qualities the overall composition entails. In Young's notation based on a traditional language these graphical notations could even fertilise the dialogue towards the design team and dancers as part of the project.

Within the studio the graphical elements sometimes start to directly extend to the actual physical space, as it was the case for example in the "Angle of Incidence" event in Madrid in 2011 where the movement lines that formed the overall dynamic of the events of 24 hours became as well a visible 1:1 scale graphic within the large extensive floor area of the Venue. In the XYZ's events of 2017 the graphical elements of notation extended even further across the media, from the physical floor to the moving parts of the installation, to projections and video layers of the event.

Creative accounting

As important as the creative elements for developing a project are, without generating new funds or controlling a realistic budget none of the projects would be possible. Hence, an adaptable approach to finances is very important, with and without existing external funding or grants. Sponsorship in kind, ranging from material to technical support is always needed and we manage to gather this substantial support always before the next academic year starts.

If you apply for an EU fund, which we did for the international "Bauhaus Lab" collaboration, you need at least two years in advance to bring all the different disciplines and partners from various institutions together and to create a sustainable and holistic cultural agenda. We managed to receive for the proposed international network of interdisciplinary laboratories funding by the European Culture Programme. Our main Partners were Institutions in Budapest, Marseille, London, Jena and Weimar.

For that year the AAIS programme had a substantial budget and we needed to work with it in an appropriate manner, as each position was assigned to a position within the project and could not be transferred over to another. Even whilst the decision-making process in the collective changed the ideas for the applied project over time, the budget was static and not flexible to change for the new proposed concepts. Even within this strict EU-regulated administrative framework, we managed, without this ever being an ambition or aim of the work in the first place, to build the biggest building, with a minimal budget, in the shortest time with students who mostly did not come from an architectural background. At the end this project did show that **only with the combination of the partners coming from academic and cultural institutions, working intensively together with the collective of student, experts, and educators it was possible to implement the interprofessional project in this format.**

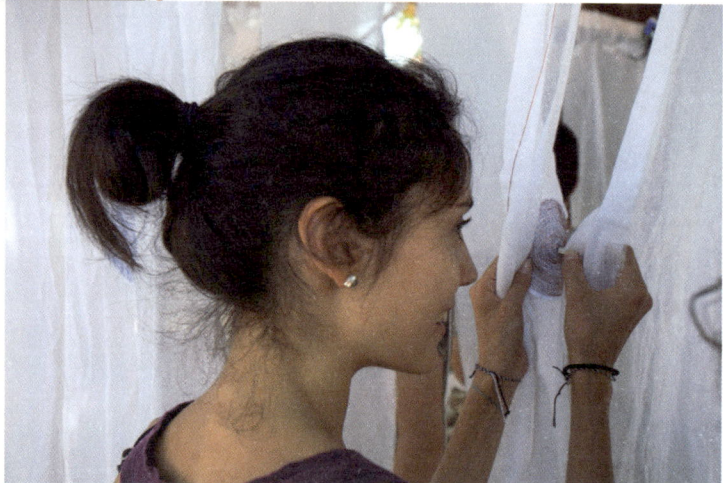

6.28/29/30
Testing sound and notations with
Distractfold Ensemble at the Architectural
Triennale in Lisbon in 2013. (SY/VB)

6.31
Working with 'low budget constructions' using left over materials at the "Seed to Scene" festival. (TS)

6.32
Reusing existing structures as framework for AAIS constructions during for the Angles of incident project at the Matadero Madrid. (TS)

6.33
Use of leftover plywood, fabric and ropes for
lightweight structure and canopies. (TS)

6.34
Testing structure for
Cologne Events. (TL)

When we talk about projects emerging out of a 'low budget constructs' we also generated projects without having 'no budget' at all. In these cases, we would depend even more on outside collaborations and in-kind support. We used leftover materials from other activities to develop our projects in that way that their overall value was not compromised. This structure has in some cases a clear advantage in organisational and administrative terms, as where no budget is flowing, the accountability is purely concentrated on the product and project itself rather than monetary liabilities. Working with limited or no budget can certainly present challenges, however it can also create creativity and resourcefulness. By utilising leftover materials or donations from others, you can reduce costs and potentially create something of value without compromising the overall quality of the project. The absence of monetary liabilities can simplify the organisational and administrative aspects of the project, allowing you to focus solely on the creative and productive aspects of the work. However, it's important to keep in mind that even without a monetary budget, there should still be a clear plan and accountability in place to ensure the project's success. Communication and transparency with collaborators and stakeholders become even more important in making the project a success.

These examples describe the methods we follow in our processual working practice. With various activities that bring people together for an exchange and discourse, promoting the student's work and creating a productive and innovative atmosphere for all involved actants. Of course, there are many more stories to tell as our approach is an ongoing process for applied teaching and learning developments.

References
Cage, John (1969) "Notations", Something Else Press, New York
Cunningham, Merce (1968) "Changes: Notes on Choreography", Something Else Press, New York
Guest, Ann H. (1974) "Labanotation: The System of Analysing and Recording Movement" Theatre Arts Books, New York
Miller, Leta E. (2001) "The Musical Quarterly", Vol. 85, No. 3, Oxford University Press
Patterson, Thomas W. (1968) "The Time of Roland Kayn's Cybernetic Music"
Tschumi, Bernard (2005) "Event-Cities 3: Concept vs. Context vs. Content", MIT Press Cambridge, MA

Theo Lorenz
Tanja Siems

COMPASSION, COLLABORATION AND CREATIVITY

We believe compassion is the basis of each collaborative work. The ability to sense the needs of others and the will to work and stand up for each other is the most fundamental starting point of each creative process.

Besides social and organisational skills, ethical behaviour and considerations play a fundamental role in the effectiveness of a creative process as we create and design the future we want to live in.

Responsibility in Design

Ethical behaviour here goes beyond the collegial behaviour, as the impact of the actions of the project extend beyond the direct team of collaboration. With each project we address tangible issues that impact a wider group of actants or circumstances at the location of our intervention and beyond. We need to be aware of this impact and the responsibilities that arise out of these matters of concern unfolding around the immediate network. The need for careful ethical approaches became very apparent in the projects we did in Covent Garden in London, at the Matadero Madrid and in Cologne at the DQE (Design Quarter in Ehrenfeld), where the impact of the changes in old-established neighbourhoods were evident and new forms of common ground were needed to re-establish communication. Equally, a high level of cultural sensitivity was required in projects within political settings, such as "ReSet Barcelona".

If we want to thrive as individuals within an ensemble of other subjects and objects one needs be able to navigate a wide spectrum of opinions and positions. The individual aim needs to be reached through negotiation and shared experience rather than top-down decision-making, but at the same time one must be able to take responsibilities and to step up. Both require from us a deep understanding of one another. In other words, one has to be compassionate in order to be able to collaborate and create effectively.

Compassion as an act of creativity

Immanuel Kant sees the German 'Mitleid' – 'com'- 'passion' or 'co- suffering' as doubling the suffering as one suffers alongside the original sufferer (Kant 1788). Martha Nussbaum on the other hand states that compassion is the basis of our social construct, however she reads compassion as separate from reason and based on emotion (Nussbaum 1996).

Hannah Arendt was critical of compassion as a basis for political action, arguing that it could be harmful to the public sphere and undermine the potential for genuine democratic engagement. She believed that compassion was a private emotion that was not suited for the public realm of politics, which required rational deliberation and collective action based on shared interests and values (Arendt Chapter 5 1998).

We, however, do not distinguish compassion from action and thus see compassion as a passionate act of togetherness. It is seen here as a behaviour, that enables us to act together, create tangible results and avoid, or even remedy, suffering or injustice. Aristotle's belief that compassionate action was not just about feeling pity or sorrow for others, but about actively working to help them in a way that was appropriate and effective can still be seen as a basic principle of compassion today. In regard to collaboration, he believed that compassion was necessary for building and maintaining strong relationships with others, as it helped to create a sense of mutual understanding and support. He saw compassion as a central component of a flourishing human life and argued that cultivating compassion was essential for living a good and virtuous life (Aristotle and Roger Crisp 2014).

Within intense and passionate project-based collaboration we often meet moments of conflicts and high levels of individual stress. Whereas, within top-down hierarchical systems this kind of friction would lead to potential repression and exclusion it has shown that an active compassionate behaviour not only alleviated the issues, but also led to astonishing achievements by all involved parties.

Whilst we should never arrive at a situation where we start to think 'Now I have to take care of myself' or consider merely 'What's in it for me?', we equally need to be aware of providing a supporting network without self-deprecation. Compassion is not only necessary for the well-being of others; it is essential to an individual's well-being.

Compassion is not a one-to-one exchange, but it is an exchange of many. If you support someone, it is not to be expected to receive the same support of the same person or group. Rather the total sum of exchanges should constantly grow to a network of support.

More often than not we could see that team members of the studio found themselves in personal difficulties when met with help, inclusion, and empowerment, did not only repay the favour to their peers, but excelled in collaborative tasks and personal work, lifting up the entire network.

Therefore, compassion is one of the main ingredients for being able to work creatively together. Compassion, in distinction to mere empathy, is always linked to actively engaging with the ones around us, identified injustice and causal issues.

The many words that are thrown around now are manifold; all try to hint in the same direction of understanding others. However, whatever word we use, compassion, empathy, sympathy, sensitivity or understanding, all are meaningless if not coupled with action. It is not enough to say, 'I see you'. It is essential to say, 'I will take action with you'. Most importantly, compassion recognises the intrinsic causal relations of problems without equalising them.

Finding creative solutions, not out of pity, but by understanding that advocacy and activism will create a better environment for all. Artists and Creatives can lead compassionate movements through their way of working.

Don't look away

The recognition of patterns that cause harm and addressing them with active interventions that counter them is imperative for creative work in the way we define it. No one can claim all the solutions, or to always act with infallibility. However, all actions can be frustrating if they merely add to the underlying problems that cause suffering.

The first step here is to seek to understand the full spectrum of circumstances and to enable oneself to 'see'. This approach requires us to first unlearn to look away and suppress elements of the overall network and instead learn to look ahead and act. We seek to live in a world that creates and does not destroy. In turn, this means we ought to actively avoid any level of violence. Accepting any level of violence or discrimination desensitises one to accept further levels of injustice or violence. It all returns to us.

Learning to 'look away', even for things that are deemed normal or even necessary in our societies, causes us to suppress compassion and empathy. There are many areas of daily, normalised forms of violence, against nature and other living beings, yet many build up a seeming rational defence to overcome and suppress this knowledge, and in some cases society tells us, in varying ways and in different parts of the world, that some form of violence is normal and necessary. Individuals build up arguments like culture and personal well-being to defend their behaviour. Many become downright defensive when reminded of the simple fact, that despite all of the justifications, one would have to accept violence and pain in order to 'enjoy' the result.

Othering

Once we learn to accept basic forms of violence, we become gradually desensitised against more severe levels of violence and injustice. Level by level, we accept or look away if other fellow human beings are treated differently with violence and discrimination. This ability of 'othering' or even 'dehumanisation' has been built up in human history over a long time. The power of the few over the majority depends on it. You can only wage war if you convince your soldiers that the enemy is other; you can only colonise if you tell your society that the occupied are lesser (Quijano 2018); you can only have a patriarchy if you tell men that women are weaker (Hooks 2013). We have come a long way in debunking these former 'norms'.

We are now at an inflexion point, where old powers try with all force to regain their lost ground as highlighted by the United Nations Development Programme in the 2020 report on the example of global gender inequality (UNDP 2020). Society is now more than ever aware of injustice, racism, misogyny, environmental dangers, and animal welfare.

A global, almost panicked, push-back has started with populism, accelerated by conspiracy theorists and authoritarians who think themselves born to great power. It's important to work creatively against these forces, to keep creating awareness from the roots up. Compassion needs to be the new normal. Once we have recognised potential or actual injustice, violence, or opportunities for avoiding situations and bettering existing ones, we should find creative solutions through advocacy, design, and creation. These will have a lasting effect leading incrementally to societies that are more just.

Fields of intervention

Considering the enormity of the issues of today, one might ask what we can actually do to create awareness and action that help to work against these forces. As with so many complex topics, there is no single answer or recipe we can apply. However, we believe, that every individual and collective can forge areas of interventions that not only are compassionate but start to create in turn as well as new initiatives and projects. The studio with its students, educators and collaborators tries to always apply compassionate behaviour, that is aware of unconscious bias, discrimination, and personal well-being. A few areas of intervention can be described within the setting of the studio in more detail: Besides a general approach towards collegial teams the applied briefs of the year's topic are set out to challenge questions of our times. The projects themselves are used as common grounds for different parties to participate in and through plant-based culinary experiences moments of enjoyment and togetherness without compromise that eschew even basic forms of violence.

Project Briefs

Over the years we aimed actively to operate within this ethos and address these issues through the academic course brief and the related seminars, projects and workshops. In consecutive briefs titled "Trust, Truth, Integrity", "The art of resistance", "Others" and "Scream out loud" we addressed issues of disinformation, othering, injustice, and exclusion. We ask questions of identity in briefs such as "Wherefore art thou" and "The Three Graces?" and "The Estranged Gaze of Compassion". These project briefs formed the basis for an open discussion ground and approach to design and offered the opportunity to research, develop and act within the specific set of locations and networks of the year. Over the years the examples of this approach of the work did not only manifest within the main events it became even more apparent in the contextualising research and activities in relation to the events.

'Common Ground', Intellectual Empathy and 'After-effect'
We seek to create through our projects a common ground between maybe otherwise disconnected parties. Culture is a platform to meet through shared narratives and values, without preconceptions or conditions.

A form of study within social science describes this form of critical thinking as Intellectual Empathy. With approach, each individual is asked to question one's social identity, social differences and beliefs in order to overcome conscious or unconscious biases and enable oneself to empathise with the situation of others on a critical and intellectual basis. In this way, areas of commonality and consent can be identified and form the basis of a common ground (Linker 2015).

Compassion in all its aspects in itself is a form of collaboration between individuals. As in any form of productive collaboration it is important to see it as a process of preparing the ground for further development to take place, rather than to try to set an outcome from the outset.

Art and design can take advantage of the creative, thoughtful space to identify and reveal problems, finding applied solutions to solve them. If I can empathise with the needs of a client, I am more likely to find a solution for said client that fulfils the given tasks. If we are sensitive to the talents, strengths, and weaknesses of our collaborators, we are more likely to create an outcome that lifts the entire team and creates meaningful work.

Compassionate behaviour continues beyond the timeline of an immediate project or interaction. Compassion has no end date. With this in mind the measurement of success of a project should not only be the direct impact they have in the short run, but we should observe and re-evaluate constantly what the impact of our work has been over the years. Our definition of after-effect relates to that of Andrew Benjamin. Benjamin describes the after-effect not merely as a nostalgic matter or a memory, but as the way we understand the world around us and its place in time and thus after-effect is needed to understand our present.

We share Benjamin's view that the after-effect is not just a personal or subjective experience, but something that is shared collectively. He suggests that the after-effect is a kind of residual presence that remains in the world after an event has taken place, and that it can be felt or sensed by anyone who is attuned to it. It highlights the fact that the past is not something that is simply over and done with, but something that continues to shape our lives and the world around us in profound ways (Benjamin 2010, pp 29-47).

The after-effect can be measured on multiple levels, from the impact on individuals to a wider impact on groups, businesses, or parts of society. Equally we can see what physical transformation has occurred through design interventions. The after-effects might have been planned and envisioned, or purely serendipitous. The impact is rarely easy to pinpoint, as the after-effects depend on a multitude of various factors, vary in scale and duration and quality, and diverge in multiple directions synchronously. To care and to keep an active communication with the involved networks over the years is essential.

> The first area of evaluation for us as an academic course is to see the impact the studio and projects had on our alumni. We can see and observe how many of them apply the interprofessional ethos in businesses, education, and their personal lives. Students have set up successful businesses worldwide, ranging from Chicago to Seoul, Beijing and Sydney. Working across different disciplines, they teach in countries like the UK, Greece, Israel, Bangladesh and Indonesia. Furthermore, they initiate performances, festivals and projects across the world, winning prizes, grants and awards. Most importantly, we can see that they keep working within collaborative networks and extend these networks constantly, continuing and developing a compassionate, collaborative way of working.

The next area of after-effects we looked at was the network impact our projects had. What lasting connections have been created and how did these develop. A clear example of this is the "Seed to Scene" project in Covent Garden. For this project we can trace the overall actor network of individuals and groups, but equally that of design artefacts, building and even organisation back to the event itself. At this event we started collaborating for the first time with New Movement Collective, David McAlmont and Andy Dean, all still collaborating and working with us today and developing unique approaches in performance and design since.

> We can trace the origin of our used material, reused, recycled or 're-appropriated' and see how they are used still today. The furniture created from left-over material is today still used across different institutes, the wooden walls transformed after several exhibitions and iterations into external planting pods in a private London Garden and the 'hexa-dress' has become a permanent part of the AA's archive after having been used in several shows and presentations. The Venue, back then a disused building in the middle of Covent Garden, has since returned to a permanent creative use as a film school.

The largest scale of impact might be measured towards the social and political frameworks we have worked within. We must ask ourselves the question whether our projects did indeed support a compassionate togetherness, helped to generate understanding and discourse as well as mediating among its stakeholders. This was important to apply within the various projects we did at the cultural centre Matadero in Madrid, where we helped to create a permanent weekly market for local produce, or later at the Xue Art Museum in Beijing where new links for creative and educational programmes where initiated.

7.1/2
Culinary experience during "Angles of Incident"
with "Olivia te quida" at the Matadero Madrid
during creative exchanges and discussions. (VB)

7.3
Culinary plant–based buffet
during "Trust, truth, integrity"
at the Testbed two. (TL)

Culinary Cultures

With a complex and contagious topic such as compassion it is difficult to cover all areas and topics that needs discussing. We might not have personal agency or cultural references, conflate entirely separate topics, or simplify experiences of others. To create a common ground in such a situation it helps to demonstrate the framework of thought through a topic one can directly influence, explain, and show causal relations and outcomes of a compassionate behaviour, without indoctrination.

For us plant-based culinary experiences have been a useful platform that can demonstrate compassion and cultural togetherness in a good manner (Lorenz, Siems 2021, pp35-57). Cooking is considered a creative act due to the utilisation of imagination, experimentation, and artistic expression to transform raw ingredients into a finished dish. Cooking involves a combination of technical expertise and artistic creativity, and we can use our creativity to devise new recipes, experiment with flavour and texture, and present dishes in visually appealing ways. Cooking also provides a high degree of personalisation, as each individual cook can add their own unique touch to a recipe, customising it to their personal taste and preferences and in this way, cooking can be a highly expressive and emotionally fulfilling activity, offering an outlet for artistic exploration and self-expression.

In addition to being a creative act, cooking also has a strong connection to togetherness and social bonding. The act of cooking and sharing food has long been a way for people to come together, share stories, and build relationships. Cooking for others is a way to express care and hospitality, and sharing meals can create a sense of community and belonging. We see cooking as a collaborative activity, with individuals working together to create a shared meal or dish. It requires us to pool resources, divide tasks, and working towards a shared goal, promoting a sense of teamwork and co-operation.

Cooking in this way we have done culinary events as part of our projects from London to Spain, Germany, Italy and Spain, bringing people together to enjoy, discuss and interact. With food we can respond to culture, social grouping, and behaviour. We can trace the origin and process of the ingredients from their origin to the recipe and plate and can show local roots and environmental relations. With plant-based food we can show a compassionate and aware way of cooking and eating and most significantly we can create a moment of togetherness and enjoyment within a creative setting. Importantly, we don't lecture about animal welfare or environmental impact during these events, but rather aim to create a positive experience for everyone involved. We hope to convince through example and evidence at hand, managing to excite renowned chefs and gastronomes as well as initiating many discussions on cultural impact and personal well-being.

The self-righteous trap

It is important to note that compassionate does not imply making oneself 'better', but society. If one feels superior to others by doing the right thing, it results in falling back into the same conundrum: if one is better the other has to be lesser; hence, the right act is no longer an act of compassion, but a new form of othering. This othering would bring the entire process back to where we started. It would create renewed oppositions, suppression and violence from all sides. Compassion needs to be driven by its after-effect, not only on us but on others as well. This is what distinguishes active behaviour from cult subscription, radicalisation, religion, and political posturing. Compassion depends on acting not merely being.

It is a fine line and difficult balance to keep. Individuals have to learn how to advocate without becoming preachy or extreme. Let's learn how to push the boundaries of compassion without suffering or suppressing our own needs. Let's create strength without force. Let's learn true compassion and create a more equal environment for all. We can learn to show empathy and compassion, even to the uncompassionate in power, whilst simultaneously withholding compassion from arcane systems. If we don't truly understand those that stand against innovation, how can we persuade them or those that follow them that new ways of co-operating are possible.

In this way, it should not be the aim to gain 'power' or 'take over' as that would cause in turn, again, the need to maintain said power or suppress others. The model here instead would be to constantly find consent and thus avoid a system of top-down power. This is an important and substantial part of any relationship, be it collaborating or living together. All too often we have seen how revolutions were turning into autocracy, no matter how righteous their initial cause was. The cycle of gaining power and keeping power necessary only to be rightfully overthrown in turn, is hindering progress and development.

As creators working in collectives, it is essential to recognise the urgent need to counter the global push-back against compassion and empathy, which is fuelled by populism, conspiracy theories, and authoritarianism. We actively can create work that reflects the complex realities of our world and promotes empathy and understanding across different communities. By collaborating and sharing our creative resources, we can amplify our voices and make a more significant impact in promoting awareness and inspiring compassion in our audiences. We can harness the power of our diverse perspectives and experiences to tell stories that resonate with a broader audience and challenge prevailing narratives of division and hatred.

The Creative fields have the unique position to be able to advocate for those who can't create, speak up, or decide through their work. We can create through our work a common ground for equals in a constant discourse to create a more just society. It is vital for us as a collective to be mindful of our own privileges, biases and assumptions and strive to create work that is inclusive and reflective of the diversity of our society. By doing so, we can contribute to building a more equitable and just society that values the dignity and worth of every individual, regardless of their background or beliefs.

We want to create a society that is truly inclusive, where everyone has an equal voice and an equal opportunity to succeed. This will require a commitment to social justice and human rights, and a willingness to work together across different sectors of society to build a better future for all. By embracing compassion as the new normal, we can build a brighter and more equitable future for ourselves and for generations to come.

References
Arendt, Hannah (1998) Chapter 5, "Action", The Human Condition. University of Chicago Press
Benjamin, Andrew (2010). Writing Art and Architecture. Re:Press, Chapter: "The Work of After Effect" Pages: 29-47.
Aristotle and Crisp, Roger (2014). Nicomachean Ethics. Cambridge University Press, Cambridge
Kant, Immanuel (1788) Critique of Practical Reason, Translated by Lewis White Beck, Bobbs-Merrill, NY.
Linker, Maureen (2015) Intellectual Empathy: Critical Thinking for Social Justice. University of Michigan Press
Lorenz and Siems (2021): SRL Publisher, Association for Urban, Regional and State Planning "Food and the City as planning fields of action" article "Cooking up Ideas – Culinary Interventions"
Martha Nussbaum (1996) Compassion: The Basic Social Emotion, Social Philosophy and Policy 13
Quijano, Anibal (2018) The Coloniality of Power: Notes Toward Two Decades of Decolonial Thinking. Duke University Press, Durham, NC
United Nations Development Programme (UNDP). (2020). Tackling Social Norms: A Game Changer for Gender Inequalities. UNDP.

7.4
"Parding your Beggon" provoking intellectual empathy during the "Moult" festival at the Teatro Aberto in Lisbon. (AR)

7.5
"Spatial erformance Festival"
at the Romantso in Athens.
(TL)

7.6
Audience interaction through live performed
sound and choreography at the "Space" in London
as part of the "Moving Stone" series. (VB)

8

Amr Assaad
Theo Lorenz

SPACES OF OPPORTUNITY

A Home for /People

A /person is someone who is at home in more than one discipline, whose professional identity is not singular but made up of many forms, each refined, each in dialogue with the others. This text focuses on where such /people find their home, what kinds of spaces acknowledge and accommodate a practice that moves between genres, institutions, and forms of knowledge. They are not switching between roles but living a composite practice that challenges traditional boundaries. If their work spans disciplines and genres, where can they find spaces that not only recognise but actively support this complexity? Where do they locate the opportunities, not just for presentation, but for meaningful collaboration, experimentation, and continuity? And what should such opportunities entail, if they should truly reflect the practice of /people? This raises a key question: where then, is their home? What kind of space, physical or professional, can contain and support such a plural identity?

When we think of artistic spaces, we often picture something provisional, vacant buildings re-purposed into studios, situated on the urban fringe. While such places offer affordability, they often result in isolation. Located away from central areas, they limit access for both artists and audiences. This can lead to narrow networks, with projects developed and shared within closed circles. For those working across disciplines, this restriction poses a challenge. What these spaces seem to lack is openness, not only in terms of architecture, but in access, attitude, and infrastructure. If creative people are to thrive in their work and find one another across boundaries, the question we need to ask is: what kinds of space are enabling, supportive, and generous?

Framing a New Environment

A broader framework is needed. How can artists access advanced tools, not just tools in the generic sense, but those that meet professional standards, both technologically and qualitatively? Tools that allow artists to not only realise their ideas but explore and expand them in unexpected directions? How can they connect with people who contribute not only skills but also critical input, collaboration, and production support? And how can they access networks, not merely social circles, but transformative links and initiatives that extend their capabilities, resources, and reach? Networks that operate in the Latourian sense, where both people and things, institutions and tools, collaborate to shape creative outcomes? To answer these questions, artists need what we can call spaces of opportunity. These might be studios, workshops, clubs, rehearsal rooms, cafés, or even virtual

platforms. But what makes them matter is not just their physical form. A space of opportunity transforms the work, it enables creation at a level that would not otherwise be possible. It creates extended possibilities for collaboration and wider visibility. These are spaces defined by the quality of tools, the clarity of structure, and above all, the generosity of the people who sustain them. Spaces where trust, curiosity, and shared enthusiasm are the starting points, not the exception.

Many artists are already used to assembling their working environments across different places, constructing a patchwork of collaborators, infrastructure, and audiences. The Interprofessional Studio at the Architectural Association (AAIS) in London is one such space. As the home base of the studio, it offers a working environment where art can be generated, rehearsed and shared with a small but immediate audience. Its strength lies in its openness and continuity. However, it cannot exist in isolation. For the work to evolve beyond the internal circle of AAIS, it must be extended outward, into applied spaces of opportunity, where professional tools and wider networks can actively shape and scale what is being developed inside. In this way, the AAIS studio becomes a crucial node in a larger constellation, one that supports both deep research and outward exchange.

Making and Meeting

But making the work is only one side. Just as important is where that work meets others, where it becomes visible, open to interpretation, critique, and collaboration. These moments of encounter are not only about audience engagement but about creating conditions for future work: opportunities for conversation, the discovery of unexpected overlaps, the meeting of potential collaborators, and the extension of shared networks. These interactions can carry the work beyond its initial presentation, generating lasting impact and long-term relationships.

Traditionally, the public reception of work happens in fixed venues: galleries, theatres, concert halls, museums. These institutions remain important, but for work that crosses disciplines or defies categorisation, their fixed structures can feel limiting. Their frameworks are shaped by inherited categories and protocols, visual art is displayed, theatre is staged, music is performed. Often, the emphasis is on finished work, neatly packaged and temporally contained. There are clear lines between artist, audience, and institution. While such clarity has value, it can exclude modes of working that are open-ended, conversational, or in-process.

If we want to create space for the unfamiliar, we need venues that are as agile and open-ended as the practices they support. This doesn't mean a lack of structure, but a willingness to be reconfigured. Architecture, in this context, plays an active role, not as neutral background but as a vital actant within the network of subjects and objects. A space's form, texture, history, and light, its layout, circulation, or acoustics, can constrain or invite. When a space allows for re-reading and re-use, it transforms itself and the work within it. It becomes co-creator.

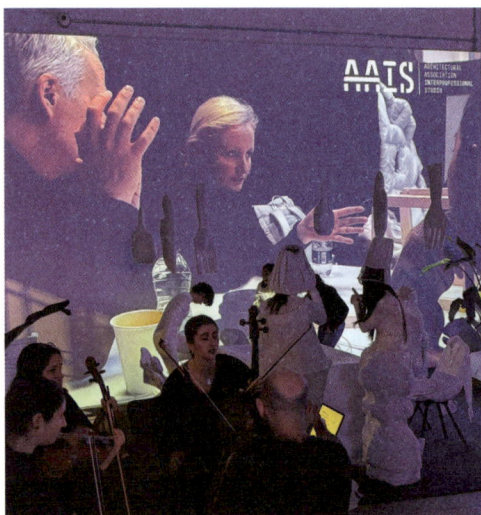

8.1/2
Creative talks and discussions during our Festival
BORNE: "To those born later" created and presented by
the AAIS Studio at the Shoreditch Arts club London (HK)

8.3/8
BORNE festival at SAC: Rehearsal
of the "Non-normativity" scene,
Music by Daniel Pukach (TS, TL)

8.4
BORNE festival: Rehearsal for
"The Inside World" scene at the
Shoreditch Arts club in London (TL)

The Architectural Association itself was founded in exactly this spirit. In 1847, a group of students, disillusioned by the hierarchical and rigid models of architectural education of the time, created their own institution. They literally found a space together, outside the conventional structures, and began to reshape how architecture could be taught and learned. (Macarthur, 2010). This impulse to claim space and redefine the terms of practice continues in the work of the AAIS today, where disciplines meet and new models are tested.

Re-imagining the Club

Throughout recent history, some of the most powerful spaces of opportunity have emerged not from official institutions or defined programmes, but from socially constructed environments that allowed for overlap, exchange, and reinvention. One of the most iconic examples is Andy Warhol's Factory in New York. The Factory was not just a studio, it was a convergence point for artists, musicians, writers, performers, and cultural outsiders. Its loose structure and open social rhythm encouraged spontaneous interaction, unexpected collaborations, and creative crossovers. It was a space that generated new work by enabling people to encounter each other across disciplines. In this sense, it was not simply a host for creative activity, it actively transformed it. The Factory represents an early and now legendary model of what a space of opportunity might be when it becomes central to a network of exchange, visibility, and risk (Colacello, 2014).

In 1985, another influential model emerged in London: the Groucho Club. Formed as a counterpoint to traditional private clubs, the Groucho carved out a relaxed environment specifically for people working in the arts, writers, performers, visual artists, musicians, who were otherwise peripheral to elite cultural institutions. What made the Groucho effective was not just its clientele, but its deliberate informality. This was not a casualness without consequence, but a structured openness: a space of permission, where ideas could emerge out of conversation, where unplanned overlaps led to tangible creative outcomes. It did not look or act like a cultural venue, but for many, it served precisely that function. It became a site of connection and emergence, and as such, an engine of artistic life (Patten, 2015).

These historical examples are not to be romanticised or copied but understood as part of a lineage. Today, as creative work becomes increasingly fragmented, spread across genres, disciplines, platforms, and unstable economies, the role of such spaces is more necessary than ever. For /people working across boundaries, spaces of opportunity are essential not only for production but for connection: places to try, to listen, to find allies and audiences, and to generate work that might not have otherwise emerged.

Within our network, a key task has been to identify and nurture these current-day equivalents, spaces that support work-in-progress, spontaneous assembly, and interdisciplinary friction. Places where informal encounters carry real professional value, and where overlaps between /people lead to the start of initiatives that might unfold over months or years.

Spaces like Shoreditch Arts Club inherit this logic, not by replicating the Groucho or the Factory, but by rethinking what cultural and professional proximity might mean today. Here, the social is not a separate domain from the professional, it is where shared purpose begins.

Contemporary Collaborations

Recent collaborations include Hope Alkazar and Xtopia in Istanbul, MAMO Centre d'art de la Cité Radieuse in Marseille, and Shoreditch Arts Club in London. Each of these spaces represents an exceptional example of a space of opportunity, distinct in form and approach, but unified by their professional standard, cultural relevance, recognisability, and strong embeddedness within wider networks. They are not only hosts for creative practice but active contributors to it.

Hope Alkazar occupies a central pedestrian zone in Beyoğlu. Its spatial openness and cutting-edge technological infrastructure support large-scale, immersive, multimedia projects. Its visibility and accessibility invite a broad spectrum of publics, enabling artistic interventions to unfold in dialogue with the urban environment.

MAMO, owned and curated by French designer Ora Ito, is situated on the rooftop of Le Corbusier's iconic Unité d'habitation. The former gymnasium, re-imagined as a platform for contemporary art, merges iconic architecture with experimental contemporary practice. MAMO has hosted many significant artists who work against or in dialogue with this modernist masterpiece. Its elevated setting and symbolic location offer both conceptual and literal visibility, turning the rooftop into a stage for artistic confrontation and innovation.

Shoreditch Arts Club operates as both a social club and a cultural venue. It is not oriented around prestige, but around possibility. Its transparent ground-floor façade lets the city in; it refuses opacity. Visitors are not filtered but welcomed. Inside, every interaction is shaped by personal attention: bar staff who know the artists, technicians who engage directly with their process, curators who listen. Events unfold not only in programmed form but through spontaneous, informal overlaps. It is a space where people feel recognised, not just admitted.

Hope Alkazar is similarly open. It offers professional-grade equipment, over twenty high-spec projectors, motion-tracking systems, a suite of audiovisual technologies, but just as critical is the openness of its team. Tutors, students, artists, and technicians work collaboratively and non-hierarchically. During "Love Has Never Been...," a project focused on the legacy of James Baldwin, this collaborative ethos enabled an experience that was not immersive in the generic sense, but immersive in its urgency, emotional intensity, and thematic coherence.

8.5/6/7
BORNE festival: Rehearsal of the
"LOOP" scene at the Shoreditch
Arts club in London (TL, TS, TL)

8.9
Exhibition opening, revealing the design journey
and aspects of the BORNE festival performances
at the Cité Radieuse de Marseille (TS)

Through their individual strength, spatial configuration, and cultural presence, each of these sites becomes more than a venue. They act as transformative agents within wider networks, nodes that extend the capacity of /people to share, evolve, and expand their practice across contexts.

Infrastructure and Invitation

These examples show that a space of opportunity is built not just through design, but through atmosphere and intent. Atmosphere, in this context, refers to the feeling of being welcomed and recognised, an important condition for /people to feel at home. It is the social quality of a space that invites presence and return. Intent is what reinforces this atmosphere: it is expressed through spatial layout, programming, team dynamics, and the values embedded in the daily running of the space.

Equipment matters, artists need tools they might otherwise never access, but so does the context in which those tools are made available. High-quality infrastructure is essential, but it becomes truly valuable when integrated into a socially engaged and open environment.

A good space does not merely offer resources; it invites interpretation. At Shoreditch Arts Club, the boundaries between performance, conversation, and installation are fluid. One might encounter a projection while queuing for a drink or find themselves part of an impromptu talk in the kitchen. These moments are not distractions, they are invitations to engage. The club becomes a shared environment, shaped by everyone who enters. Its model of spatial clarity and social permeability reflects a deep integration of conceptual and lived experience, emerging from a team closely involved in both the development of these ideas and their practical, real-world application.

This was evident from the club's very first public event, a collaboration between artist Peter Spanjer and musician Loshh. Spanjer, whose practice had long involved sound and moving image, used the event to explore how performance could reshape the relationship between these elements. The club's spatial conditions, its layered architecture, audiovisual setup, and intimate scale, allowed for the creation of an immersive world where the visual and sonic intertwined. The trust and familiarity between the two artists underpinned the risk-taking involved: together, they ventured into new territory, using the club not simply as a venue but as a site of expanded practice (Shoreditch Arts Club, 2023).

Hope Alkazar, while spatially and culturally different, offers a parallel example. It combines technical excellence with a proactive and collaborative ethos. Its infrastructure, ranging from advanced audiovisual systems to integrated motion-tracking technologies, is state-of-the-art. But its defining quality lies in how this infrastructure is embedded in a team that is culturally alert, socially engaged, and organisationally generous. Artists, tutors, and technicians work together in a space where professional rigour and openness to experimentation coexist. The team's involvement in wider cultural conversations and political currents makes the venue not just a platform but a partner.

These are not just well-equipped or flexible venues; they are active contributors to the creative process. For /people, this matters deeply. They require not only freedom and time, but also structured frameworks through which to build work and connect it outward. They need places where chance encounters and focused inquiry happen simultaneously. This combination, of openness and form, of tools and temperament, is what allows for real dwelling. Informal workshops, shared meals, and lingering conversations are not secondary to the work; they are integral to its unfolding.

Together, Shoreditch Arts Club and Hope Alkazar represent what happens when infrastructure, intent, and atmosphere align. These spaces show what a 'space of opportunity' requires: shared curiosity, trust, and enthusiasm that becomes a collective gain for all involved. Everyone, organisers, producers, technicians, artists, and wider communities, contributes to shaping the environment. This collective spirit is what transforms a venue from a place of presentation into a site of active creation and meaningful connection. Both venues are exemplary hubs of people who support, communicate, and embrace emerging practices. Their engagement with current cultural and social conditions makes them transformative spaces, not only for the artists they host but for the networks they activate. These collaborations leave lasting after-effects, for institutions, individuals, and the works themselves, setting the stage for what Latour describes as the ongoing process of re-composition (Latour 2010). This kind of time-rich, socially embedded structure is rare, and essential.

Designing for Plurality

The architecture of these spaces is not invisible. In fact, its clarity is part of what allows for improvisation. At Shoreditch Arts Club, the spaces are distinct and singular. The rooms don't fold away or shift mechanically. Instead, each space is designed to do one thing well. Paradoxically, the more a space tries to accommodate everything, the less usable it becomes, turning into an idea of flexibility rather than a place of action.

8.10/11/12
BORNE festival final preparations for the
open Rehearsal, venue MAMO Centre d'art
de la Cité Radieuse de Marseille (TL, TS, TL)

Yet while spatial functions are clear, the aesthetic is loose. The club feels like a collage. It is layered with objects, textures, and contributions from many hands. Artworks hang alongside vintage finds and ephemeral artefacts. There is no singular author. The result is not chaos, but composition, a dynamic mix that encourages new readings, new moods, and new uses. As one might describe it, it is 'maxy-clashy', a generous clash of materials and identities that creates a space people linger in, inhabit, and influence.

This principle is reflected in the AAIS project "Borne," held at Shoreditch Arts Club in 2024. It was a series of performative events exploring inherited privilege, human empathy, and the ethical future. With minimal formal staging and multiple moments of audience interaction, the work unfolded fluidly across the space, making use of the club's layered architecture as both frame and field.

Similarly, the interdisciplinary festival "Love Has Never Been..." presented by AAIS at Hope Alkazar in Istanbul, showed how architecture and advanced technology can become expressive agents. Using motion, choreographic objects, spatial sound, and video mapping, the performance asked whether freedom is a given or something made. Spread over three days, the event included workshops, performances, and a rehearsal with audience. The architecture of Hope Alkazar, a central venue with multiple overlapping functions, enabled a layering of movement, sound, and reflection that shaped the audience's experience of the themes.

Latour's notion of composition fits here. In his Compositionist Manifesto, Latour proposes a shift from the critical dismantling of structures toward the assembling and sustaining of connections between heterogeneous actors—human and non-human, spatial and symbolic. Composition, in this sense, is not a flattening of difference but a dynamic integration of distinct elements into provisional, adaptable wholes. It extends and updates Actor-Network Theory by foregrounding the practical work of keeping networks alive, responsive, and co-productive (Latour 2010).

For /people, this concept is particularly resonant. Their practices are composed of diverse skills, platforms, and disciplines. They work within constantly shifting conditions that require not just adaptation, but active re-composition—testing, remaking, and aligning their methods and collaborators anew. In spaces of opportunity, this becomes visible. The work is not presented as finished, but unfolded, questioned, and re-formed. These venues do not stabilise the work—they offer frames in which it can continue to evolve.

In this way, structure becomes a partner. The more specific the parts, the more interesting the combinations. People do not perform *in* the architecture; they perform *with* it.

/Person and /Practice

This principle applies not only to space but to people. The /person, like the /space, is not a blank slate, but a defined practice that remains open to dialogue and transformation. This means that a /person does not arrive in a space empty-handed, but with a body of knowledge, a mode of working, and a set of standards shaped through the accumulation and navigation of multiple disciplines over time. A musician, architect, or choreographer brings their own language. In dialogue, they do not dissolve that language, they test it. In doing so, they extend their practice.

/People are not singular identities, but complex assemblages, composed of interlinked skills, materials, collaborators, and techniques. Their practice is shaped in motion, in collaboration with others, and it grows through exchange. Meeting others, especially within spaces of opportunity, is crucial. It is here that /people encounter new initiatives, face other perspectives, and allow their methods to be challenged or extended. Practice is not fixed; it emerges in relation. It is built over time, through conversations, through rehearsal, through critique.

Spaces of opportunity enable this. But this possibility also depends on the people who maintain and animate the space. The team, its curators, technicians, coordinators, and support staff, forms a vital part of the network. Their openness, responsiveness, and belief in the work are not peripheral, but central to what makes a space re-composable. The presence of an alert and engaged team allows /people to extend their practice without losing its shape. They help hold a frame that is flexible but not formless.

These spaces offer enough clarity to orient, and enough openness to surprise. They create the possibility for mutual recognition, where different practices can meet without collapsing into sameness. This is not about hybridity for hybridity's sake. The goal is not endless flexibility, but mutual transformation, where each practice remains visible and coherent, but becomes more expansive through contact with others. This kind of working takes time, trust, and a willingness to be surprised.

The /person is also a composition, a shifting alignment of human and non-human actors, methods, histories, tools, and sites. As with architectural space, the work of practice is not to settle into fixed roles but to remain in motion: tested, remade, and continually re-composed.

Economic Structures and Generosity

Generosity is a foundation, but it must be sustained. A space of opportunity cannot rely solely on good intentions or improvised support; it must be backed by economic frameworks that are both resilient and purpose-driven. At Shoreditch Arts Club, this foundation comes from Buckley Gray Yeoman's architectural studio, whose backing enables a consistent level of professionalism and cultural continuity. Hope Alkazar, sustained by Nike, combines advanced infrastructure with civic-minded programming. In both cases, commercial support does not dominate the identity of the space, it remains largely in the background, enabling the cultural mission without dictating its form. What is visible, and what defines the atmosphere, is the presence of the host and the team: the people who activate the space day to day. These partnerships show that commercial and cultural aims can align, when guided by shared values and long-term vision. What makes these models effective is not just funding, but the responsiveness to artists, the trust built with communities, and the alignment with the evolving intentions of the space.

8.13/14/15/16
An explorative derive around the Unite
directed by Tanja at MAMO Centre d'art de la
Cité Radieuse de Marseille (TS, TL, TS, TL)

What matters is that economic stability does not compromise openness. A space of opportunity is not only defined by its architecture, programme, or funding model, but by the people who make it work day-to-day. The commitment and presence of partners, collaborators, and especially the core team are integral to sustaining generosity. These individuals embody the values of the space and translate its intentions into daily action. Their long-term investment, combined with institutional or commercial support, ensures that generosity is not a one-off gesture but an ongoing capacity. Openness becomes a shared responsibility, not only in terms of access but in how ideas are welcomed, challenged, and transformed. Too often, arts spaces must choose between access and survival. A true space of opportunity must be both viable and generous, so opportunities can be given. This requires clarity of purpose and trust in the communities that use it.

At the centre of this social and economic ecology is the host. Not a manager or a gatekeeper, but a mediator, someone who listens, connects, and adapts. The host does not impose their vision but holds the conditions for others to unfold theirs. This is particularly crucial when working with emerging or experimental artists. Paths are not linear. Ideas shift. The host navigates needs, balances logistics with intention, and links people who might not otherwise meet. In spaces like Shoreditch Arts Club, this role is central to how the network operates. Artists are not left to chance encounters, they are actively and thoughtfully introduced to one another and to collaborators beyond their immediate framework. This includes connections to curators, producers, or potential commercial partners. These introductions often widen artistic networks and open up new possibilities, not only for creative development, but for economic sustainability and long-term relationships. The result is not just successful projects but living systems of exchange. The host, in this sense, becomes an active part of the composition, someone who extends the possibilities of the space through interpersonal alignment and cultural care

Timeliness and Context

A space of opportunity is not defined only by its location or infrastructure, but by its moment. Timeliness matters because the relevance of a space is not fixed—it is relational. A space becomes a space of opportunity when it responds to what is happening around it, when it meets a need or amplifies a question already present in the world.

The AAIS event *Borne* at Shoreditch Arts Club took place in its inaugural year (AAIS 2024). With five extensive segments, the event tested and re-appropriated the architecture, atmosphere, and operational model of the newly opened space, connecting it to a new network of emerging practitioners and conversations. The performance not only tested Shoreditch Arts Club's spatial setting but significantly extended the relational field of the AAIS studio.

215

The festival *Love Has Never Been...* in Istanbul was equally timely (AAIS 2025). Presented at Hope Alkazar, it reflected on the legacy of James Baldwin and the concept of freedom. Its themes became even more urgent as political protests and public unrest unfolded in the city during the festival itself. The alignment of artistic inquiry and civic context created a heightened sense of urgency and resonance—for artists and audiences alike.

Other examples illustrate this interplay of space and moment. At Matadero Madrid, the AAIS event coincided with the opening of a newly activated part of the former slaughterhouse site. At an important stage in its transformation into a cultural district, AAIS helped establish a common ground for exchange between local communities and new publics. At Drydon Street in London, a long-disused cultural building was temporarily revived amidst the encroaching commercialisation of the area, reasserting its cultural potential. In Elberfeld's DQU, an area where local communities and developers had largely ceased to engage with one another, the AAIS project reopened a space for shared conversation and collaborative potential (Siems/Lorenz 2023).

Recognising such moments requires alertness from the host, the team, and their partners. Their sensitivity to context allows them to seize fleeting opportunities and translate them into meaningful encounters. These moments, while temporary, leave traces, they extend the network, deepen relationships, and contribute to the evolving composition that defines a space of opportunity.

Continuity and Composition

When a space of opportunity works, people feel at home. They are able to make work, test it, and share it. They encounter others, build relationships, and begin things that outlast the moment.

These spaces are not about singular achievements but about continuity. Their power lies in re-composition, returning to the same places, people, and ideas with fresh eyes and new energy. Nothing is static. Networks expand, connections deepen, and previous experiences are reactivated in new configurations.

As Latour reminds us, change happens through the interplay of human and non-human actors, through active composition, not isolated invention. The work is never finished but always unfolding.

Spaces of opportunity are where that unfolding begins.

References

Colacello, Bob (2014). *Holy Terror: Andy Warhol Close Up*. Vintage.
Latour, Bruno (2010). 'An Attempt at a Compositionist Manifesto'. *New Literary History*, 41(3), pp. 471–490. Johns Hopkins University Press.
Macarthur, John (2010). *The Picturesque: Architecture, Disgust and Other Irregularities*. Routledge.
Shoreditch Arts Club (2023). *Peter Spanjer × Loshh*: https://shoreditchartsclub.com [Accessed 8 Apr. 2025].
Siems, Tanja (2023). *Imparting City: Methods and Tools for Collaborative Planning*. Basel: Birkhäuser.
Patten, Alice (2015). *Groucho 30th Anniversary*. London: Groucho Club.

Project AAIS 2023-24, Event series "Borne", Defeng Li, Hanying Zheng, Hsiang-Ting Huang, Jiaanqi Cheng, Keyi Huang, Kexin Ou, Mohan Chen, Mincan Li, Nandini Jadhav, Siyu Yang, Siyu Yang, Svasti Agrawal, Weizhi Wang, Xingjiang Hu, Xuemeng Xuan, Yan Jiang, Yifei Chen, Yixiaoxiao Han, Yuan Chang, Yunyi Ye, Zhenni Wen, Zhijia Hu, Architectural Association School of Architecture (AA), London
Project AAIS 2024-25 Event series "Love Has Never Been..." "Mennatallah Mohamed, Tianyue Shao, Hui Fan, Maria Perdomo, Junjian Wang, Yue Fu, Shalu Liu, Eilyn Cheung, Shuren Li, Jinyu Li, Architectural Association School of Architecture (AA), London

8.17
AAIS introductory performance rehearsal by Wa-ju Ekeji
with James Baldwin related dramaturgy at the Istanbul
venue Hope Alkazar within the Xtopia programme. (TL)

8.18
"Love Has Never Been ..." set within the cutting-
edge technological infrastructure of the
Istanbul venue Hope Alkazar. (TL)

8.19
Alice E. Chapman, Alice Herzog, Aklisa Kociu, Lydia A.M. Punch
with Mennatallah Mohamed and Maria Perdomo performing at
the AAIS Istanbul festival "Love Has Never Been …" (TL)

8.20
Alice E. Chapman, Alice Herzog, Aklisa Kociu, Lydia A.M. Punch
with Mennatallah Mohamed and Maria Perdomo performing at
the AAIS Istanbul festival "Love Has Never Been …" (TL)

8.21/22
AAIS Istanbul festival "Love Has Never Been …" with
live music performed by Daniel Pukach, Lucy Gijsbers,
Johan Höglind and Martha-Maria Mitu. (YF)

ACKNOWLEDGEMENTS

With this /people publication we are showing our gratitude to all our AAIS tutors* and external examiners Richard Wentworth CBE, Prof. Kelly Chorpening, Prof. Barbara-Ann Campbell-Lange, Robert Taylor, who were sharing their endless knowledge with us.

A big thank you to all our AAIS students from the graduate diploma, the post-grad diploma and the MA and MFA degree-programmes, who created over the last years the following projects "Bauhaus Lab" (2009), "Seed to Scene" (2010), "Exquisite Corpse" (2011), "Angles of Incidence" (2012), "Flow Fields" (2013), "The Conversation" (2014), "Moving Stone" (2015), "UnREAL: XYZ" (2016), "Trust Truth Integrity" (2017), "A Walk" (2018), "Portrait of Humans" (2019), "Scream out loud! "(2020), "Origin: The story of Us" (2021), "Echo: Wherefore Art tough" (2022), "Moult: Three Graces" (2023), "Borne: The estranged gaze of compassion" (2024), "Love Has Never Been … "(2025). Special thanks to our AAIS alumni Yuyang Cheng, Zoya Currimbhoy, Raluca Grada, Dongsoo Koo, Lumia Liu, Tuo Lin, Elyssa Sykes-Smith and Zoie Jie Wang, who helped us over the last years.

Thanks to Christian Küsters and Mihaela Mincheva at CHK Design in London for the art direction and design of this beautiful book, and for many years of interesting graphic design discussions and great collaborations ranging from the AAIS logo to the interactive webpage design.

An immense thank you to our Sponsors and Partners, who were collaborating with us and our AAIS network over the last years, especially to Christina Smith OBE and her Foundation for the remarkable space in Covent Garden and Ariadna Cantis and Pablo Berástegui for hosting us at the Matadero Madrid various times.

Many thanks to Benedetta Tagliabue "The Fundació Enric Miralles" for including us in the ReSet Festival in Barcelona, to Will Alsop and his team for having us at their educational retreat "Las Heras", in Girona, to Stefano Rabolli Pansera and his "Mangia Barche Gallery" on Sardinia and to Javier Peña Ibáñez, for accommodating us at the "Concéntrico" international architecture and design festival in Logroño.

Special thanks to Hope Alkazar and Xtopia Istanbul and their team, especially Günsu Sari, Akalan Lalin, Melike Mucahit and to Melike Altinisik, Founder of MAA architects and MAALab, for establishing the connection to the venue. Special thanks to Ora Ito and his team for having us at the Marseille Modulor, MAMO Centre d'art de la Cité Radieuse, the contemporary art centre at Le Corbusier's iconic Unité d'habitation building in Marseille and to Amr Assaad and Matt Yeoman the Shoreditch Arts Club founders and their team for having us at the SAC in London.

Thanks to the "Bauhaus Lab" team at the Theaterhaus in Jena, Markus Heinzelmann with Jan Brüggemeier, Janek Müller and Éva Kozma at the c3 Centre for Culture and Communication in Budapest, as well as Nick Crosbie the founder from Inflate and Steve Webb co-founder from Webb Yates Engineers for helping to build a stunning structure with us, and the AA Foundation team Miraj Ahmed and Saskia Lewis.

Thank you to Sabine Voggenreiter and her DQE-team at the "Design Quartier Ehrenfeld", Andreas Schmitz and Judith Mayer from the "KunstSalon Stiftung" Foundation in Cologne, the Lisbon Trienal de Arquitectura team "Close, Closer" with Beatrice Galilee, José Esparza, Manuel Henriques and to Maciej Switała of the INAW Krakow international Biennial.

During the pandemic lock down in Europe we had great help from Dongsoo Koo and his Gallery team in Seoul and the Yue Art Museum in Beijing to make our AAIS live performances happen, thank you. Thanks to the Roca Lisboa and Roca London Gallery, as well as the team of the Coin Street Community at the Oxo Tower Wharf and the LabTech team in Camden Market in London for their support. Thanks to the team of the Romantso, the creative hub and cultural centre in Athens and especially to João Lourenço, Vera San Payo de Lemos, Célia Caeiro and their team at the Teatro Aberto in Lisbon and to Mark Morris at the Victoria & Albert Museum in London.

Thank you to all photographers for their documentation of the AAIS events, especially Farah Aly (FA), Parastoo Anoushehpour (PA), Valerie Bennett (VB), Yue Fu (YF), Oliviu Lugojan-Ghenciu (OG), Takako Hasegawa (TH), Jason Kofinas (JK), Dongsoo Koo (DK), Theo Lorenz (TL), ArchLabyrinth studio Athens (AL), Hadar Menkes (HM), Alexandra Radounikli (AR), Tanja Siems (TS), Patarita Tassanarapan (PT), Zoie Jie Wang (ZW), Henrietta Williams (HW), Sue Jan Yeong (SY) and Tuitui Zhang (TZ) for their wonderful images we used in this publication.

AAIS tutors* Argyris Angeli, Jan Brüggemeier, Mona Camille, Nerma Cridge, Andrew Dean, Malgorzata Dzierzon, Jonathan Goddard, Heiko Kalmbach, David McAlmont, Kyriaki Nasioula, Pierre Nedd, Joel Newman, Gemma Nixon, Patricia Okenwa, Mauricio Pauly, Thomas Parkes, Yoav Ronel, Noa Segev, Hila Shemer, Patarita Tassanarapan, Tony Thatcher, Atimanyu Vashishth, Joe Walkling, Steve Webb and Renaud Wiser, co-founder of the AAIS programme Theo Lorenz and Tanja Siems.

/people

AT HOME IN MORE THAN
ONE DISCIPLINE

PUBLISHED BY
Actar Publishers
New York, Barcelona
www.actar.com

AUTHORS
Theo Lorenz
Tanja Siems

EDITED BY
Theo Lorenz
Tanja Siems

GRAPHIC DESIGN
Christian Küsters
Mihaela Mincheva
chkdesign.com

**WITH CONTRIBUTIONS
BY / CO-AUTHORS**
David Greene
Miraj Ahmed
Albena Yaneva
Robin Hunt
Portia Kamons
Graham Harman
Amr Assaad

**COPY EDITING AND
PROOF READING**
T Lorenz, JJ Purtill

PRINTING AND BINDING
Gràfiques Jou, Barcelona

DISTRIBUTION
Actar D, Inc. New York, Barcelona

New York
440 Park Avenue South, 17th Floor
New York, NY 10016, USA
T +1 212 9662207
salesnewyork@actar-d.com

Barcelona
Roca i Batlle 2
08023 Barcelona, Spain
T +34 933 282 183
eurosales@actar-d.com

ISBN
978-1-63840-192-6

LIBRARY OF CONGRESS CONTROL NUMBER
2025937972

PUBLICATION DATE
September 2025

COVER IMAGE
©Sue_Jan_Yeong

The publisher/author/editor has made every
effort to contact and acknowledge copyrights
of the owners. If there are instances where
proper credit is not given, we suggest
that the owners of such rights contact
the publisher which will make necessary
changes in subsequent editions.